"Finally! A guilt-free guide to everything moms feel guilty about. Wise, warm, witty—and full of grace. Perfect for women in every season of insanity!"

—Jane Rubietta, speaker and author of *Grace Points: Growth and Guidance in Times of Change*

"As a homeschooling mom, wife, author, attorney, church member, and more, people often ask me, 'How do you do it all?' My honest answer is, 'Not too well!' I frequently bobble one or more of the many balls I have in the air, but now I have a flock of new ideas! Barbara's new book, *Help Wanted for Busy Moms,* is a delectable compendium of practical pointers to make all of life go more smoothly—from housework to health to friendships. Barbara takes us on an engaging, often humorous, journey to help us find the balance and peace so desperately needed by today's moms."

—Christine Field, author of *Help for the Harried Homeschooler, Life Skills for Kids, A Field Guide to Homeschooling, Should You Adopt?* and *Coming Home to Raise Your Children.*

"For every mom like me who wonders how other women keep their countertops clutterless, children well fed, checkbooks balanced, and still find time to laugh with friends, grow in faith, and smile at life, Barbara Mang offers simple secrets for success."

—Nancy Guthrie, author of *Holding on to Hope*

"Finally, a book that can actually help us pull together all the loose ends and responsibilities in our overloaded lives! Barbara has created a truly practical book that assists every mom in her desire to bless and encourage her family. It's the perfect handbook for handling the joys and stresses of motherhood."

—Karol Ladd, speaker and author of *The Power of a Positive Mom* and *The Power of a Positive Wife*

"'How does she do it?' is a question we've all asked at one time or another as we've admired (and envied) the seemingly effortless accomplishments of friends, neighbors, and other women at church. Barbara Mang is not a superwoman. She lives in the real world—like most of us. But she's discovered some practical, doable strategies for creating a home that's a place of peace and nurture...for mom and everybody else."

—Elizabeth Cody Newenhuyse, former editor,
Moody magazine; author and speaker

"The title is incomplete. This book is not for moms only; it is for us men too. I, who cook nothing more complicated than toast, skipped the recipes, but everything else in this book is fascinating and marvelously useful. Before you have read many pages, you will like Barbara Mang and trust her for sound, practical tips on homemaking and parenting. You will ask for her telephone number.

"This is not a preachy book, but it helped me see some of my shortcomings, especially lack of organization."

—Donald Cole, radio pastor,
Moody Broadcasting Network

"Barbara has written a kind and encouraging book filled with real stories, practical pearls, relatability, and spiritual substance. She delivers hope for even the most crazed mom to be able to bring order to her chaos—whether that chaos be in her home, in her busyness, or in her head.

"This book has a wonderful warmhearted feeling...I believe it will be a soothing balm to weary-souled, bleary-eyed moms."

—Charlene Ann Baumbich, speaker, humorist,
and author of the Dearest Dorothy series

Help Wanted
for Busy Moms

BARBARA MANG

HARVEST HOUSE PUBLISHERS

EUGENE, OREGON

Cover by Left Coast Design, Portland, Oregon

Cover images ©: Steve Cole/Getty Images/Photodisc Green; Siede Preis/Getty Images/Photodisc Green; Ryan McVay/Getty Images/Photodisc Green

Backcover author photo © Bill Bilsley

HELP WANTED FOR BUSY MOMS
Copyright © 2004 by Barbara Mang
Published by Harvest House Publishers
Eugene, Oregon 97402
www.harvesthousepublishers.com

Library of Congress Cataloging-in-Publication Data
Mang, Barbara.
  Help wanted for busy moms / Barbara Mang.
      p. cm.
Includes bibliographical references and index.
  ISBN 0-7369-1265-7 (pbk.)
  1. Mothers—Religious life. 2. Mothers—Conduct of life. I. Title.
  BV4529.18.M36 2004
  248.8'431—dc22   2003020630

Printed in the United States of America

04 05 06 07 08 09 10 11 12 / VP-KB / 10 9 8 7 6 5 4 3 2 1

In loving memory
of my sister, Sally, and my mother, Dorothy,
both of whom died during the writing of this book.
Each was an inspiration to me and also a wonderful mom.

Acknowledgments

I'd like to thank my three children—Carolyn, Andrew, and Steve—for providing me with so many wonderful memories, a few of which have made their way into this book.

I'd also like to thank my two advance readers, Kay Tooze and Sue Cornman, whose valuable comments made this a better book. And this effort wouldn't have been possible without my extended family and many friends who have shared their lives and experiences with me, enriching my life and providing me with material.

I also want to thank Janis Long Harris, from whom I've learned so much about writing and publishing, and last but certainly not least, the wonderful people at Harvest House who have made this book possible—Terry Glaspey, Carolyn McCready, Barb Sherrill, Betty Fletcher, and Kim Moore.

I'm very grateful to all of you.

Contents

This Job's for the Birds!

෯ ෯ ෯

The other day I sat on my back porch watching a mom or dad robin (I can't tell them apart) picking up twigs I had trimmed from my silvery Russian sage plant. Evidently it was nest-building season, and the bird picked up one sizable twig and started to fly away. Then it seemed as if she looked back at the remaining twigs, and they just seemed too good to pass up. She grabbed another twig in her beak, and another and another. She now had four seven-inch twigs clasped in her beak. When she tried to fly them away to her under-construction home, she could barely get off the ground and wound up dropping a couple of the twigs before she could take off.

Her industrious activity reminded me of my own attempts to do just one more thing, to save steps, to make every minute count. Like the robin, I have tried to carry too many bags of groceries into the house from the car and dropped a half-gallon of what quickly became spilled milk. I have piled items at the foot of the stairs to take up on my next trip to avoid wasting time going upstairs, only to have someone stumble on the items, breaking things and becoming annoyed at my blockade as well.

Like that robin, I often don't know when to say "enough." One more task or responsibility looks tempting to get done at the moment. *Why make an extra trip*, the bird probably thought (do birds think?), *when I can just as easily take four twigs as one?* But the time she used up in trying to cram four twigs into her mouth and complete her liftoff probably exceeded that needed for four calm and orderly trips to the nest. There's nothing wrong with multitasking, but when it's overdone, it can be counterproductive.

All of us mothers work hard the way mother birds do. Whether our children are infants, toddlers, school children, or teens, and whether or not we also work outside our homes, motherhood involves work—often joyful work, to be sure—but work nonetheless.

Throughout my years of motherhood—and my three children are now all teens—I have found that by trying to simplify and organize, I can more easily handle my tasks. I'm not naturally a superorganized person, which might be the reason I have found it necessary to figure out some shortcuts. But when I take the time to plan a little bit and to combine jobs when possible, I find that I can stay sane and accomplish more. I have also learned that when I skip prayer and Bible reading in order to stuff in a little more activity for the day, all my accomplishments ring hollow.

Another observation about birds is that they don't seem to feel guilty the way many mothers do. I know stay-at-home moms who think they really should have a job outside the home even if the family budget doesn't require it. And I know working moms who feel guilty about being away from their children while they work. Other moms don't always feel all that maternal and wonder if they are really in the right occupation (motherhood). They feel guilty about those doubts. Mother birds don't seem encumbered by guilt feelings, but mother humans do. I hope this book can somehow ease your feelings of guilt and increase your freedom to simply be who you are: the friend, wife, mother, and woman God made you to be, different from other women because you are—yourself! You don't have to be like the mom who loves to bake cookies every day or the corporate executive mom who manages both career and family. By relaxing, reducing, or eliminating guilt and finding some ways to simplify, you can be free to enjoy your life and family and make the contribution that is uniquely yours, relying, as the birds do, on God's care. "Look at the birds of the air, that they do not sow, nor reap nor gather into barns, and yet your heavenly Father feeds them. Are you not worth much more than they?" (Matthew 6:26).

I've been a stay-at-home mom, an employed-outside-the-home mom, a married mom, a single mom, an affluent mom, and a poor mom. In this book I've tried to be real, touching on many of my experiences and struggles, and on some victories as well, so you would know that I have had many of the problems you have (and maybe more or fewer), and you might find some encouragement from the fact that I have survived them—issues like depression, divorce, and financial reversals.

I'd especially like to thank my friends and family who've shared their lives and ideas with me and will find themselves in this book. They know the hilarity of my writing about household organization, cleaning, and scheduling, and they'll smile as they realize that these ideas are the result of the (usually) cheerful chaos that seems to pervade my home.

I hope the ideas in this book will help you feel less frazzled, calmer, and more satisfied with the big and important job you do all day, every day, serving as the heart of your home.

1

A Place for Everything?

Taming the Housework and Organizing Your Home

❧ ❧ ❧

I learned a valuable household organization technique from my friend Carla one day while I was having lunch at her house.

I said, "Carla, your kitchen always looks so neat and orderly. Where are those piles of paper I seem to always have on my countertop and desk?"

"I learned this from Marty, and it works every time," she said. "When you're having company, get a brown paper grocery store bag. Take it to your desk and dump the huge stack of papers into it. Open a closet and put the bag on the floor. Shut the closet door. You will probably never even miss those papers."

I have employed this useful hint time and time again in the years following Carla's helpful example. She followed up her advice by sending me several books on home management with titles like *Tidying Up for Harried Moms, If You*

Can't Identify the Contents, It's Time to Clean the Fridge, and *Spring Cleaning: Bring Out the Bulldozer.*

But unless I'm having company, I still have piles of papers. I don't save old newspapers and just one or two magazines. I get rid of junk mail as soon as it comes. I have applied numerous principles from the books Carla's given me. But my paper mountains still accumulate. Kids' school papers and forms, mail requiring action, bills, catalogs I really need something from, to-do lists, and more.

And speaking of paper, while there's an abundance of it in the kitchen, we never seem to have any in the bathroom. I'm convinced my children take showers and then dry off by mummifying themselves in toilet paper from head to toe. That's the only way we could go through the number of rolls we do. And while my children are all intelligent, they somehow cannot master the workings of the toilet paper holder. Not one of the three can work it and install a new roll. I am the only person in our household who ever does it.

So I seem to have paper, paper, everywhere—except where I want it, of course. This chapter will offer some concrete ways to simplify your chores and gain, at least temporarily, that wonderful feeling of being organized. And I promise that the ideas will be more substantial than the grocery bag technique!

Clearing Out Clutter

Nothing messes up my house as quickly, or as easily, as paper—piles of newspapers, mail, school papers, forms to fill out, and receipts seem to grow faster than the weeds in my garden. Even in this electronic age, most of my activities are still paper-based. I used to worry that as soon as I threw something away, I would need it again (and this indeed has happened). But that is rare, and by starting a folder for "keepers," I can drastically reduce paper clutter and still retain necessary items. As I ruthlessly overpower those stacks of paper, my house stays neater and I don't feel overwhelmed by ever-growing paper mountains.

Tackle your biggest pile of magazines, newspapers, or junk mail, and go through it quickly and mercilessly with a goal of decluttering your home. Remember, you can probably reread that unforgettable article again at the library or online.

If you don't already have one, label a file folder "2004 Taxes (or whatever the current year is)." Then you can toss all your receipts from your purse, as well as bill stubs that have tax ramifications, into the folder for sorting and use after the end of the year. Label another folder "Bills to Be Paid" and put it in a convenient place where you can easily add incoming bills for payment twice a month. Another important folder is "Warranties and Instructions" for all appliances, equipment, and toys your family owns because, if all else fails, you can always read the instructions!

The average U.S. household receives
24 pieces of junk mail per week, more
than 1200 items per year.

Another Clutter Killer

Entering a child's closet—even when the child is still young—is an eye-opening experience for a mother. When my son Steve was about five, I opened his closet door to hang up his church clothes and found artwork penned in permanent black marker all over his closet walls. I was surprised, but I remember thinking how considerate it had been of him to do it in the closet and not on the living room walls.

Although I knew my daughter was a pack rat without even entering her room, hers was the kind of closet you really should approach wearing a helmet and being prepared to run when you open the door. Everything from dried-up cereal bowls to unmatched shoes to gum wrapper chains would try to escape their unpleasant confinement when they had the chance. I must admit that she might have inherited this "dangerous closet" gene from me.

A great place to declutter is a child's closet. Go through the contents of one shelf at a time, sorting outgrown clothing into a pile to donate to charity and receive a tax deduction. Fold and replace the remaining items on the shelf, stacked in piles of similar items. Be sure you have a large black garbage bag with you for broken, sticky, or otherwise objectionable materials. Repeat this process with other shelves as time permits.

A Heart for Art

By now you know how I feel about piles of paper—I dislike them. But some papers are more endearing than others. I can cheerfully toss catalogs, junk mail, and old newspapers into the recycling can, but I find it nearly impossible to part with one of my children's masterpieces. This sentimental attachment led to several large cardboard boxes of school and artwork being uselessly stored in the attic. I saved some of the papers in scrapbooks and photo albums, but all moms know the vast numbers of beautiful paint, chalk, hammered metal, cutout, and glued on drawings in various sizes that even one child produces during his educational career.

Here's a solution that provided an added benefit besides decluttering. Using pushpins, I hung the children's artwork all over our finished basement, nearly covering the walls completely. I didn't frame them or do anything fancy. Except for a world map, which I considered important, nothing but their pictures appeared on the walls. Not only did I eliminate the attic boxes, but the children were also very pleased that I thought enough of their artwork to display it in such abundance in a frequently used area of our home. Other kids who came over enjoyed seeing the display as well, and several moms told me that their kids had asked if they could decorate their basement the same way.

If you want to increase your child's self-esteem, enjoy the pictures those little (and bigger) hands made, and also reduce the number of your storage boxes, try this inexpensive but effective decorating technique.

ᔕᔕ ᔕᔕ ᔕᔕ

> Out of clutter, find Simplicity.
> From discord, find Harmony.
> In the middle of difficulty lies Opportunity.
> —ALBERT EINSTEIN, *Three Rules of Work*

To-Do Lists

I have several to-do lists. My Main List is the one that I check every day. It is handwritten on 8 1/2 x 11 paper, preferably green, pink, or some color I can recognize amid the many other papers I have around the house. I've tried typing up my list on the computer and printing it out, but for some reason it just doesn't seem like my good old list anymore when it looks so nice.

My Main List contains everything I want to get done in the reasonably near future: make eye doctor appointment, take insurance policy to safe deposit box, send note to Sandra. It's helpful to group tasks such as errands, phone calls, and paper-handling activities. My list contains usually about 20–25 items, and I cross them off as I do them, recopying the list when it becomes mostly crossed out and messy. I'll admit that it includes some items, like wash all windows, which are recopied again and again onto new lists without being done.

I sometimes make a Today List, choosing a couple of things from this Main List and adding other things that must be done today. (Since I love words and word play, "Today" was a fun knockoff on "to-do" for me.)

Then I have my Long-Term List, which includes make curtains for the porch, paint living room, and buy new rug for family room. My Long-Term List even includes save for and buy new (used) car.

I have one more list, and it's attached to the refrigerator with a magnet. Every time I run out of a kitchen staple, I write it on my Grocery List so I don't forget to buy it next time I'm at the store.

When I have something down on paper, I feel better because I know I won't forget it, unless of course I lose my list!

Woven Wonders

My friend Kathleen collects beautiful Longaberger baskets and uses them all over her house for decoration as well as organization. She uses them in each room to hold and organize everything from napkins to CDs to her daughter's jewelry. Here are a few more uses for baskets, and they don't have to be the expensive variety to do the job:

- rolled up towels

- extra rolls of toilet paper

- soaps

- toiletries

- logs for the fireplace

- candles

- books

❦ scarves

❦ boots, shoes, hats, and gloves

❦ toys

❦ hobby materials

❦ kids' arts and crafts

❦ bills to pay

❦ cooking utensils

❦ pencils and pens

❦ centerpieces

Edible Art

One year our family entered a gingerbread house contest. We worked on our house for several days, rebaking the gingerbread walls until they came out crack free and eating all the failures. I made a stiff white frosting with egg whites, and we diligently glued the pieces together and then stuck on all the candy decorations. We even made a little curving path to the front door with M & M "stones" and dyed coconut green with food coloring for our grass. We were pretty proud of our masterpiece and optimistic about our chances of winning.

Unfortunately for us, two of the other contestants were bakery chefs whose houses featured stained-glass windows made from thin sugar candy, lighted rooms, and a doorbell that really rang. Of course, they won all the prizes.

It was fun anyway, and in the process I employed an organization method I use for many things.

I save those plastic zipper bags that blankets, sheets, and curtains come in. They make great containers for sweaters during the winter or for craft materials, Christmas decorations, or toys with a million parts. Before we started the gingerbread house, I pulled out one bag with all of our tiny Christmas trees, sleds, and wreaths to use on the project, and I loaded up all the candy and tools we'd need in another. Cleanup was easy, and we were able to quickly find what we needed the next time we were ready to work on the project.

❦   ❦   ❦

Talking Tasks

Although I often feel like the last person on the planet without a cell phone, I did invest in a cordless phone several years ago. Even better than the long stretch cords I used to have that allowed me to do a few kitchen chores while talking on the phone, my cordless allows me to make productive use of my telephone time.

Here are a few chores you can do while catching up on the latest news from family and friends:

❀ wash the fronts of your kitchen cabinets

❀ fold laundry

❀ put away groceries

❀ dust

❀ chop onions or green peppers to freeze for later

❀ wash windows

❀ deadhead flowers or pull weeds

❀ make your lunch to take to work tomorrow

This may sound obvious, but avoid chores like washing dishes or hammering nails for picture hanging because the noise on the other end of the phone will be distracting and annoying to the person you're talking to. If you've ever been on the receiving end of someone who talks to you while grinding up food scraps in her garbage disposal, you know what I mean.

Errands you can combine:

1. Drive through the bank and pick up dry cleaning.

2. Drop your child off at soccer practice and head for a nearby card shop. Choose and purchase as many birthday cards as you can afford before heading home or back to pick up your young athlete.

3. Combine trips to the grocery store and hardware store, or purchase the hardware items at the grocery or warehouse store (light bulbs, flashlight, yard tools, wastebasket).

4. Return the pants that were too short for your son. While you're at the store, find a birthday gift for his friend's party on Saturday. If you are able to afford to pick up two of the same gift, you'll be all set for the next time he's invited to a boy's party.

Dividing and Conquering Dirt

Cleaning your whole house at once requires a significant block of time. If you're like me, it's hard to set aside enough time to clean the entire house thoroughly all at once. While I don't often have large chunks of time for a big project like this, I can find shorter blocks of time nearly every day. If I take one section of the house one day and another section the next, in just a few days I can have a clean house.

To make this plan work, I divided my house into zones. My house is small, but it has four little bedrooms and two and a half small baths. I have divided it into five zones:

Zone One—two bedrooms and a bath

Zone Two—another two bedrooms and a bath

Zone Three—the living/dining room and kitchen

Zone Four—the family room and laundry room

Zone Five—the year-round porch and half bath

Try dividing your house into zones and dust Zone One today, or even Zones One and Two if you have time. By taking bite-sized pieces of housework every day or two, you can make amazing amounts of progress.

Out with the Old?

My children check expiration dates on items they find in our kitchen cabinets. Ever since 1999, when my daughter found a jar of hot red pepper flakes from the late 1980s that

I still sprinkle on my slice of pizza, she scrutinizes the cabinet contents frequently. While I believe a number of non-perishable foods have a long shelf life, and I cynically contend that expiration dates are often merely marketing tools to make consumers throw away perfectly good spices, aspirin, cookie decorating candies, and other items and purchase new ones, I have started a cabinet-cleaning routine that has reassured the children that at least I know what's in there.

You, too, can ease your children's fears of mysterious cabinet contents. Choose one kitchen cabinet, just one, where food is stored, take out all the food, wipe off the cans and bottles with a damp cloth, and replace the cabinet's contents neatly. Repeat with additional individual cabinets as you have time. And if the expiration date is older than a decade, go ahead and toss it. Your kids will be glad you did.

> Once you get a spice in your home, you have it forever. Women never throw out spices. The Egyptians were buried with their spices. I know which one I'm taking with me when I go.
>
> —Erma Bombeck

A Date with Grime

I realized something had to be done when I found myself dismantling my smoke alarm so that I could cook Christmas dinner without listening to the alarm's annoying announcement every few minutes. I was tired of fanning the gadget with a dish towel or sending one of the children to do it. I knew there was no real fire in the house, only a dirty oven that smoked when I baked butter-coated biscuits or anything else.

But what kind of example was I setting, taking the alarm apart to gain some peace and quiet and perhaps putting us all in danger by defeating the device's purpose?

You're not going to believe this, but there's no excuse for this situation because I have a *self-cleaning* oven! I just never seemed to be home long enough in one stretch to turn it on, let it do its job for a couple of hours, and turn it off to cool down so I could wipe out the ashes. The only time I really think of this chore is when I'm cooking and the smoke alarm is notifying everyone of the condition of my oven.

So I decided to set a regular appointment to clean the oven, noting it on the calendar. I chose an evening—the fourth Thursday of every month—and determined to turn on the self-cleaning function after dinner. That way I can clean the oven, wipe it out, and have the oven turned off before we go to bed. If I miss an oven appointment because I'm not home, I put an asterisk on the next calendar appointment, making sure to do it then.

I've also begun to make dates for car washing, cleaning the furnace filter, and even watering plants. Now if I can only find that calendar…

✑ ✑ ✑

Simply Clean

Vinegar is a natural substance with many uses around the house.

One time I burned several baby bottle nipples so badly in a stainless steel pan that the bottom of the pan was coated with black rubber. It looked like a Teflon pan instead of a stainless steel one. I was ready to throw the pan into the garbage when a man who was painting the living room at the time suggested soaking it in vinegar. I tried that, and the charred rubber came off easily after I soaked it overnight.

To get rid of a musty smell in the basement, saturate a washcloth with vinegar and put it in a bowl. The vinegary cloth will somehow soak up the odors and leave the room smelling clean. I now keep a vinegar washcloth on a shelf in my basement family room, and the family room no longer smells musty. I also run vinegar through my coffee maker to remove stains and pour a cupful down the kitchen sink once in a while to deodorize it. It's also good for cleaning the refrigerator and for cutting grease on dishes or empty mayonnaise or peanut butter jars you want to save. You can even use it in place of lemon juice in a recipe, and have you ever tasted those vinegar-and-sea-salt potato chips? Delicious. Vinegar also makes a good bathroom cleaner to shine faucets, sinks, and bathtubs.

Best of all, it's cheap and nonchemical.

An interesting liquid: Vinegar can be made from almost anything containing sugar or starch: fruits, grains, roots, even wood. It can be made directly from sugar, but is best made by first converting the sugar into alcohol and then turning the alcohol into vinegar.

Alcohol on Hand

My cousin Janice suggested a new painting technique that sounded great to me. I was painting spindles on the staircase, and she suggested using one of those fuzzy car washing gloves. I bought the gloves and paint, dipped my gloved hand into the paint, and went to town on the spindles. The glove cut the time of the job down considerably because it was easy to get into all the carved areas with my fingers.

But when I finished the project and took off the glove, my hand was coated with white oil paint. I made a mental note to next time use one of those thin plastic gloves you use to color your hair underneath the fuzzy glove for painting.

I had heard that rubbing alcohol is good for taking paint off your hands, is less harsh than turpentine, and is not as smelly. I applied rubbing alcohol with a paper towel, and it worked great.

Foam and Fizzle

Another basic but multitalented household cleaning item is baking soda. Putting an open box in the refrigerator helps reduce odors. Baking soda and lemon juice are great for cleaning stains from the countertop.

And one of the "funnest" things my boys ever did when they were young was what they called "making a mixture." I would let them dump in old food from the pantry, including ancient spices (if I wasn't planning on ever being able to use them) and food coloring. I'd let them add a little flour and stir the whole thing up. They thought it was great. The result was a thick bowl of usually green goop. Sometimes I'd let them make a mini chemical experiment where they poured a little baking soda in a bowl and added vinegar so that it foamed and fizzed for several minutes. They loved it.

Miraculously Clean

My friend Kay really should be an infomercial actress— at least for the soft and cuddly microfiber cleaning cloth she gave me the other day. When she speaks of the cloth's amazing abilities, her face lights up. Her enthusiasm is genuine and obvious—and contagious. I dashed home that day and did exactly what she said. I dampened one end of the green cloth, leaving the other end dry. I squeezed out the wet end as hard as I could (this is a key in getting it to work so miraculously). I then polished my bathroom mirror with the damp end and wiped off the dampness with the dry end.

Wow! It shone just like Kay said it would, with no streaks and no cleaning chemicals required.

But then I followed her instructions a little bit more. I wiped water marks off the stainless steel faucet, cleaned the bathroom countertop, and polished up the sink in a couple of minutes. She was right: This thing cleans everything! I quickly tackled some stubborn scuff marks on my natural-finish oak floors, and they came up immediately. I dusted down the wooden stairs, cleaned a couple of kitchen windows, the kitchen light fixture over the table, and the chrome on the kitchen faucet.

Don't dry them in the dryer, however. Machine wash and hang them on a rack to dry to avoid lint.

More Easy Cleaning

I've found some additional uses for my microfiber cloth, and I can't wait to tell Kay. I wallpapered my bathroom a few years ago and did kind of a sloppy job wiping off the glue before it dried. So there's dried glue on the paper in several places, and it's not easy to remove. At least it has never been easy to remove until I used my damp miracle cloth on it. Instant success—the glue is gone and the paper is still there and not destroyed by my desperate scrubbing.

Then I drove through a car wash and used the damp microfiber cloth to clean inside the car. Old coffee stains disappeared, dirty leather seats looked a shade lighter, and the insides of the windows sparkled. Of course, the next day it snowed and all my work—at least on the outside of the car—was trashed.

I used the cloth to clean salt off my shoes after walking outside, and the salt didn't reappear after the shoes dried. They almost looked as though I had polished them, perish the thought!

My final new use will surprise even Kay. I used the cloth to de-lint my black winter coat, and it worked beautifully. I might have to do my own infomercial for these cloths.

Elegant Messes

My son Steve is my "candle man." Since he was about six he has loved taking candles out of our candle drawer and setting them up for a special dinner. Of course, he often likes to use *all* the candles, so there's not much room left on the table for food, but he has a great time setting up his display. He also loves the smells of scented candles, like vanilla, although he really thinks they should make one buttermilk-scented because that's his all-time favorite smell, at least in the food arena.

But having a candle man meant there was a lot of wax to clean off of tablecloths, and the method I discovered works well for carpeting too. First, scrape off all the hardened wax you can; you may need to put the tablecloth in the freezer or rub an ice cube on the spot to harden the wax for removal. Then, put paper towels both over and under the spot on the tablecloth and iron the spot to blot up the wax. Next, spray both sides of the fabric with a stain remover and wash as usual after 24 hours. For carpet, put a paper towel on the wax and put a barely warm iron on it to soak up the wax, moving the paper around to a clean place every few seconds.

Of course, another help is putting a tray or plate under the candles to catch the wax for easier removal.

Use It or Polish It

I love using my china, crystal, and silver, and years ago I was able to buy an ornate teak china cabinet belonging to a woman from China who was moving west from Illinois to California and didn't want to take the piece with her. Nearly everyone who comes to my house comments on its uniqueness, but best of all, it holds a ton of dishes and glassware.

I'm not all that thrilled with silver polishing, but I find that the more I use my silverware, the less I need to polish it. Because my mother gave me her china and everyday dishes, I have plenty of dishes and often wonder why I continue to set the kitchen table with my chipped everyday set when I have lovely dishware going unused.

Therefore I've determined to use china at least on Sundays. Also, when each child has an accomplishment, I set his place with the red "You Are Special" plate, even though I disagree with the complete phrase "You Are Special Today," because a child is special *every* day. But that's another story.

A mind once stretched to a new idea
never regains its original dimension.
—OLIVER WENDELL HOLMES

The Lights Are On, and Somebody's Home

Most people know how to change a lightbulb, and so do I, theoretically. But I have spent literally hours changing one or two bulbs. The light fixture over my kitchen sink is encased in an old-fashioned metal frame and plastic cover that has turned yellow over the years. I'll replace it one of these days, but it works fine for now.

But when the bulb inside burned out, I spent an exasperating half hour trying to pry that wire frame off or remove the yellowed plastic cover. Finally, I gave up. The next time my friend Donna and her husband, Sam, were over, Sam asked me if there was anything I needed doing, and I mentioned the kitchen lightbulb. He asked for a knife and pried the metal frame and plastic cover down in one easy motion so that it was suspended by two wires. The old lightbulb was instantly accessible.

Another time, I worked on my old-fashioned outdoor porch lights for a very long time. I had to detach the fixtures in order to replace the bulbs. Of course, all the bulbs I had in the house were too big for the fixtures, necessitating a trip to the hardware store to find the right kind. By the time I had functioning lights again, I had logged in more than two hours on the project, but boy, what a feeling of accomplishment I had that night when my porch lights lit up the front of the house like welcoming beacons.

While I was out there working on the lights, I noticed that the storm door and windows really needed some attention. My sister-in-law Cindy told me that for cleaning windows, one tablespoon of cornstarch mixed into a quart of water does a great job. That day I only got as far as the storm door, but with new lights and a shiny storm door, I felt good about my day's accomplishment.

> ## Tired?
> So take a new grip with your tired hands
> and stand firm on your shaky legs.
> —HEBREWS 12:12 NLT

Down with Dust

My last house was new and (sort of) clean. My husband and I built it ourselves and installed the latest anti-dust and air-cleaning equipment available. Friends were always amazed that my oak floors never looked dusty, even though they knew I am far from a clean-oholic.

But my current house is 50-plus years old (nothing wrong with that!) and very dusty. Nearly every room has natural oak floors tenderly refinished by the previous owner, whose wife showed me a great mop for fast, simplified wood-floor cleaning. It is made of flat, rectangular plastic about 6" by 9" that can easily travel under beds and furniture. It came with a removable terry cloth cover that can be sprayed with dusting spray or sprinkled with a few drops of vinegar mixed with water.

In about 20 minutes, if I hurry, I can dash through my house and give the wood floors a quick once-over. The cloth can then be tossed in the washing machine and dryer to be ready for the next use.

Gearing Up for Guests

I've always been amazed when I go to someone's house as a dinner guest and, after we finish eating a wonderful meal, the hostess tucks a few items into her dishwasher, leaving her kitchen immediately neat and clean.

While I usually try to clean up somewhat as I go along simply for my own survival, after company or a big meal those helpful individuals who carry their dishes into the kitchen for me have to ask, "Where do you want us to put them?" as they survey the room and find not a single vacant spot for a dirty dish.

I've been sleuthing out how these neatniks do it, and here's what I've learned: They keep a sinkful of hot soapy water going as they cook. They simply plop dirty pans and utensils in the sink and go on about their business. In ten minutes or so they quickly wash the dirty items, rinse them, and put them away. They refill the sink as necessary to keep the water hot and clean. After the meal all they have left to handle are the plates, silverware, and serving pieces.

I don't have the system totally down yet, but at least my kitchen looks less like a war zone after dinner than it used to.

The best way to keep your daughter out of
hot water is to put some dishes in it.
—Anonymous

No-Pain Stain Removal

I always like to have white countertops in my home for brightness, even though I've drooled over some of those marble or granite ones I've seen in mixed shades of pink and black or solid dark green. But the white ones do stain easily.

All mothers have experienced stained countertops, whether the stains are from Easter egg dyeing or spilled blueberries or cranberry juice or some other substance. Along with baking soda and lemon juice, I've found that diluted bleach takes off most stains on countertops and sinks, but never mix bleach with ammonia or other household chemicals. I also use a mild abrasive cleaner for especially tough stains, being careful not to damage the finish on the countertop.

Zeros Matter

My friend Carla had a harrowing microwave experience when she put in a bag of microwave popcorn, set the timer for what she thought was three minutes, and left to go pick up her son at school, planning to have a nice popcorn snack ready for him when they returned home. But when she opened the door to the house, smelled smoke, and saw terrifying flames shooting up from her microwave, she realized she had accidentally set it for 30 minutes, just about how long she had been gone.

The very helpful firemen who arrived a few minutes later suggested not leaving the house while any appliance is running EVER AGAIN. Poor Carla—the fire even ruined the kitchen cabinets over the microwave as well as the countertop on which it sat. Imagine having to tell your husband that you destroyed the kitchen making your son an after-school snack.

In addition to carefully setting the timer on my microwave and never leaving the house when it is on, I frequently fill up a large glass or measuring cup with water, put it in the microwave, and set the timer for three (not 30) minutes. At the end of that time everything in the microwave has been steamed to smithereens, and I can easily wipe out the interior, no matter how foody it has become.

Five-Minute Phenomenon

Every time I stop by Heather's house, she has a sparkling clean bathroom. *Where's the dried-on toothpaste in the sink, the wadded-up towels, and the dusty stuff that so quickly accumulates on my bathroom floor?* I always wonder. I know she doesn't have cleaning help, and she has two active elementary school-age children. Deep down inside, I used to hope I'd one day visit her unexpectedly and find her bathroom dirty. It never happened. After observing her ever-clean bathroom for several years, I had to ask how she did it.

She told me about her Five-Minute rule, and it has eliminated the panic I usually feel when the doorbell rings. Here's how it works:

Put a roll of paper towels, a spray can of window or all-purpose bathroom cleaner, a bottle of toilet cleaner, and a toilet brush in its own stand in a cabinet in each bathroom for quick cleanups. The expense will be worth it later. Go into one of your bathrooms every day, get out the cleaning supplies you wisely stored under the sink, spray the bathtub, and wipe it out with paper towels. Spray the floor lightly and swipe it up with another paper towel. Spray the sink, clean it fast, and do the same with the mirror. Squirt in some toilet bowl cleaner, swish around the brush, flush, and replace the brush in its holder under the sink.

In just five minutes you, too, can have a sparkly bathroom whether anyone stops by to see it or not.

> The Rose Bowl is the only bowl I've ever seen that I didn't have to clean.
> —ERMA BOMBECK

A Better Bathroom

I like to keep my jewelry in the bathroom closet. In fact, this prevented it from being stolen when our house was broken into years ago (I've been the victim of three thieves, as you will learn more about in another chapter). On this occasion the thieves looked in my bedroom dresser and closet for jewelry, dumping the contents on the floor, but they failed to look in the bathroom. I didn't have much jewelry anyway, but they did get my prize feathered raccoon coat and my sterling silver.

To keep the necklaces and bracelets untangled, I screwed a number of little cup hooks into the edge of the bathroom closet shelf and they work great as necklace hangers. Old kitchen bowls on the shelves hold small pins and rings.

Shower shelves that fit into a corner and stay in place with a tension rod can be easily removed for cleaning. They tend to collect mildew (at least they do in my house), so I can take the shelves out frequently and use some diluted bleach to quickly whiten them up again before easily reinstalling them in the shower corner.

An old cabinet someone gave me provided extra storage space when I hung it on the wall over the toilet with heavy-duty bolts to keep it from falling on some unsuspecting person. I store extra towels and washcloths in it.

Sparkling Showers

All moms of older children are familiar with those long teenage showers that use up all the hot water, leaving other family members with a choice of a cold shower or none at all. We started using a timer, set for ten minutes, for each shower. Usually the next person in line is happy to police the showerer and make sure she sticks to her allotted ten minutes. Combined with staggering shower schedules for evening and morning, this has allowed all of us to leave for work or school clean and on time.

If you have shower doors that tend to accumulate water, mineral, or soap scum buildup, keep a water squeegee (like you use on the windshield of your car) handy to wipe down the doors every time you take a shower. You can hang it on the wall from a suction cup—or use that handy microfiber cloth! A quick spray of after-shower cleaner and a couple of swipes with the squeegee will keep your shower doors sparkling.

Making the most of five minutes:

1. Declutter your kitchen table.
2. Dust your kitchen and dining room light fixtures.
3. Replace bathroom towels with clean ones.
4. Sort laundry into whites, darks, and in-betweens.
5. Wash the top of your refrigerator.
6. Clean your front and back storm doors.
7. Clean pictures and frames in your living room.
8. Shake all area rugs outside.
9. Remove old food from refrigerator.
10. Gather dry cleaning and put it in the car.

Cars, Schmars

I've always admired people with cars that are clean inside and out, but my car is low on my cleaning priority list. I just never seem to get around to it unless I'm having out-of-town guests or there's so much salt on the windows that I can't see to drive (I'm just being honest here).

I remember being mortified when a little girl I was driving home from playing at our house held up a wrinkled, round, red-and-gray object and said, "Andrew's Mom, did you know there's a weird fuzzy apple under my seat?"

No, I wasn't aware of it, but as I thanked her for notifying me, I started to think of ways to keep the car cleaner with a minimum amount of work. I bought one of those garbage bags that hangs on the back of the driver's seat so the kids can (theoretically) throw things like apple cores, candy wrappers, and other debris into it. I keep old towels in the trunk, and if it rains or I'm near a drive-through car wash, I try to rinse and wipe off the outside of the car occasionally.

Another thing that helps is to turn the carpeted floor mats over in the wintertime so that the bumpy black rubber surface faces up. This way, all the mud, slush, and salt collect on the rubber, and I can simply hose it down occasionally. The carpeted sides stay unstained for use in warm weather.

Woman's Best Friend?

I am not a dog person. All my life dogs have sensed that I either feared or disliked them, so they approach me boldly with mischief in mind. When I was 12 or 13, my parents got a St. Bernard that bit my ear the very first day we had him. Our relationship went downhill from there because he had an infuriating way of resting his huge head and slobbery jowls on my lap, messing up my clothes, which teenage girls don't usually appreciate.

When my children were about four, six, and eight, we adopted a Weimaraner named Sandy. Sandy was loving and fun and utterly wild. Two of her most notable abilities were going out to get the newspaper in the morning and bringing it straight in (once inside the house she wouldn't let us have the paper until it was wet and torn), and her ability to unzip the children's backpacks and eat their lunches, leaving plastic and paper behind. After four years of our trying to make it work with Sandy, a young farm couple with another Weimaraner adopted her.

My final pet attempt was with my daughter's pit bull puppy named Lucy, a very sweet dog who refused to go to the bathroom in the appropriate place, namely outside and not in the living room. We eventually found a good home for Lucy as well.

While I admit I do not know how to handle dogs, I have learned a good method for cleaning up after them. First, blot up what you can with paper towels, standing on them to soak up all the liquid. Then mix one teaspoon of dish soap in one cup warm water, wet a clean towel in the liquid and, working from outside in, gently pat on the stain. Do not overwet. Rinse with fresh water and blot dry. Then, mix one-third cup white vinegar with two-thirds cup water and dab on the stain. Rinse with water and blot dry. The next day, sprinkle the entire carpet with baking soda, let sit a few hours, and vacuum.

Stubborn Odors

Skunks can eat flower bulbs and vegetables out of the garden, as well as stinking up the area. Anyone who has ever had a pet dog sprayed by a skunk and tried washing him in tomato juice to remove the odor knows how difficult smell removal can be.

My brother and his wife had a skunk family living under their front porch, and the smell seeped into the house. Not only did the furniture reek, but all their bedding, and even the clothes in their drawers took on that distinctive aroma. They cleaned and cleaned but couldn't get the smell out of the house. Finally, they called an air purifying company that used ozonation to fumigate the house and get rid of the smell. They had to spend a night away from the house with relatives, but the treatment worked, even on the clothes in their drawers.

If your house ever winds up smelling like a stinky animal or smoke from a fire or from years of cigarette smoking, the most effective treatment may turn out to be ozonation conducted by an air purification company and a fun overnight visit to relatives or a local hotel.

Before the Sting

While at a friend's house, a wasp stung my four-year-old daughter on the thigh. She cried very hard, and I've disliked wasps ever since. A few years ago a big colony of wasps built a nest under the edge of the roof of our back porch. They swarmed all summer and especially liked to dive bomb anyone stepping out the back door, but they hadn't actually stung anyone when I decided their time was up and I would tackle their extermination. Armed with a big can of wasp killer spray equipped to shoot long distances, I took aim right into their spot and sprayed away. After a few seconds, a few wasps dropped out and fell on the steps below. I knew there were many more inside, so I kept spraying and they kept falling out.

I repeated this process for three days, and still some rather unsteady-looking wasps continued to return to the nest. Finally, I knocked the nest down with a broom handle, sprayed it some more, stepped on it, and threw it in a tightly sealed plastic bag in the outdoor garbage can. A few days later my friend Chris came over, climbed up on the roof of the garage, and removed several more nests up there. Someone told me later that all I would have needed to do was to hang a bug-zapping machine near the nest, wait a few days, and remove the empty nest easily.

Vermin and Sloth

My friend Kathleen is a very funny person. She has that gift of being able to say things in a way sure to make others laugh. She is a beautiful redhead, and it's easy to compare her with Lucille Ball in personality, humor, and even looks.

One Saturday morning I called her to see how her preparations for her daughter's birthday party that evening were coming. I was planning to attend with my daughter.

"Oh, Barb, I just killed a rat in my basement," she said. "I'm so upset. I'm putting a sign on the door going down there saying, 'Vermin and Sloth—Do Not Enter.'" Her downstairs is a finished area with a fireplace, and the laundry room is on the lower level as well.

I laughed and asked her the size of the "rat," figuring she could probably more palatably call it a "mouse." I also asked her how she had killed it.

"I kept throwing laundry on it until it couldn't get out from under the pile. I called my dad, and he's coming over to take care of it."

Today's household tip involves catching mice. I have had several friends—single moms—who have encountered rodents in their basements or garages, and since we have no one around who can come rescue us when we stand on a chair and yell, "Eek!" we must learn the essential skill of mouse-trapping. But this is a valuable skill for married moms as well because your husband could be out of town when your infestation takes place.

Go to the hardware store and buy the tiny traps that come six in a package. Set several in the infested area by either asking your kids (if old enough) to do it or reading the instructions, using peanut butter for bait. Just be sure all children and pets stay out of the area where the traps are set so they don't get hurt.

When you come back in a day or two and find the trap with a mouse in it, simply cover the trap—mouse and all— with a plastic grocery bag and scoop it up without touching it or looking too closely. Turn the bag inside out so the trap remains inside and plop the whole thing into your outdoor garbage can or toss it down your building's garbage chute. It's good to keep setting traps until you find no more mice because they often travel in groups.

Then you can take down that sign that reads, "Vermin and Sloth—Do Not Enter!"

❀   ❀   ❀

What Do Women Do All Day?

by Marshall H. Hart, my mother's close friend from childhood (from *Home Life*, August 1976, The Sunday School Board of the Southern Baptist Convention. All rights reserved. Used by permission of author.)

Every minute, to and fro,
That's the way my hours go.
Bring me this, and take me that,
Feed the dog, put out the cat.

Standing up, I eat my toast,
Drink my coffee, thaw the roast.
Empty garbage, make the bed,
Rush to church, then wash my head.

Sweep the kitchen, wax the floor,
Scrub the woodwork, clean the door;
Scour the bathtub, then myself,
Vacuum carpets, straighten shelves.

Eat my sandwich on the run,
Now my afternoon's begun.
To the baseball game I go,
When will there be time to sew?

Meet the teacher, stop the fight,
See the dentist, fly the kite;
Help with homework, do the wash,
Iron the clothes, put on the squash.

Shop for groceries, cash a check,
Fight the crowds, now I'm a wreck!
Dinner time it soon will be.
"What's for supper?" Wait and see!

Dirty dishes crowd the sink,
Next there's popcorn, then a drink.
Will they never go to bed?
Will I ever get ahead?

"Bring me water." "Get the light."
Turn off TV, lock the bike.
"Where's my pillow?" "Hear my prayers."
"Did you lock the door downstairs?"

At last in bed, my spouse and I,
Too tired to move, too weak to cry,
But e'er I doze, I hear him say,
"WHAT DO WOMEN DO ALL DAY?"

We're Starved!

Fixing a Good, Fast Dinner Every Night

%% %% %%

When my mother was a girl in the South, the women in her family would start cooking early in the morning. They'd make a big breakfast of bacon and sausage, eggs, grits, biscuits, and more. Then they'd clean up from breakfast and start shelling peas and snapping beans and shucking corn for lunch, which they called "dinnah." They'd put on a big feast for the noon meal—ham and cornbread, fried chicken, beans, corn, fresh tomatoes, and a delicious fruit or custard pie for dessert. They'd clean up from that meal and start peeling and paring fresh peaches for peach cobbler or peach sundaes for supper. They'd fix some black-eyed peas and some okra and a chicken pie. They'd make some iced tea, and by that time everyone would be coming home to supper. And they didn't even live on a farm! This is just what they did, day in and day out, to feed their families.

Food preparation was the women's lives. My mother carried that tradition on in a somewhat modified degree, and we ate well while we were growing up. She cooked at least a pound of bacon every morning, and the four of us kids had no trouble polishing it off, mixed into oatmeal. Sometimes we'd put scrambled eggs into it—yum. My brother John loved her oatmeal and bacon for breakfast, and he still stopped by her house for it occasionally when he was in his thirties. Mother even tried making chocolate pancakes for my sister, Sally. She also made homemade yeast donuts very similar to Krispy Kremes, and the kids in our New Jersey apartment complex lined up to get 'em hot. She was famous for her potato salad with green olives in it, her apricot torte, her German chocolate cake, and homemade ice cream so loaded with heavy cream and eggs that it could've stopped our hearts with one dish. But we didn't know or care about things like cholesterol or triglycerides or low-fat.

Things have changed. Today's women, unlike many women in Mother's day, often work outside the home, and whether they do or not, the errands and carting around kids and their friends were unheard of in the past.

As a working mom—aren't we all!—I have tried to adapt some of Mother's delicious recipes to faster, healthier versions because time is short for all moms today. While these recipes aren't organic, aren't based on any particular diet or eating plan, and aren't low-calorie, they are nutritious, fast, and sure to please your family. And if you ever feel guilty about using a prepared spaghetti sauce or another convenience, remember that what you're preparing at home is likely to be a whole lot healthier than what the family would get if you just grabbed something on the way home from work or your child's baseball practice.

This chapter gives you three choices for each day's dinner, depending on how crazy your schedule is for that day. If you have the time, opportunity, and presence of mind to start a meal in the morning, by all means do so. If you have about a half hour after getting everyone home from where they had to be, use the second recipe. And if you're desperate, as I am at least 30 percent of the time, use the third recipe. These are all family-tested and meet with general approval. Some of them you'll recognize as altered versions of standard favorites women pass around between friends, family, or school or church acquaintances.

Again, the idea is to help moms not feel guilty about their cooking prowess. If cooking is your hobby and you make fabulous dishes, that's great; please invite me over for dinner. But if something else is your passion, and food is low on your list of priorities, that's okay too. If you're feeding your family nutritiously and regularly, and trying to create mealtimes that are calm and comforting for everyone, you're doing a great job. Don't feel bad if you mostly use the recipes in the "Desperate" category or if your family eats out often. No-guilt mothering will make you a more effective mom, so let guilt go and commend yourself on the good job you do feeding and caring for your family.

I hope these recipes help you fix better meals in less time and gain perhaps a minute or two for yourself. Perhaps you can use those minutes to feed your soul a brief but nutritious portion of God's Word and take a moment to pray.

ॐ ॐ ॐ

Feed Your Family Fast and Well

One of my favorite things is putting my key in the back door lock, turning it once, pushing open the door, and being greeted by a delicious smell that seems to call out, "I'm glad you're home. It's warm and cozy in here, and a nourishing meal is almost ready. Take off your shoes and relax."

A mouthwatering smell welcomes your children and husband home as well. My belief in the power of good kitchen smells was reinforced when I was selling my house. My Realtor told me that if I could bake some bread or at least dab some vanilla extract on a turned-on lightbulb before potential buyers visited my house, the smell would help them feel comfortable in my home and increase the likelihood of their buying it.

More important, of course, is creating a nurturing environment for your family, and good food smells from today's menu ideas will help.

If you can start making dinner in the morning:
Minestrone

If you have about a half hour after work to fix dinner:
Chicken-and-rice casserole

If you're desperate:
Spaghetti and bottled sauce

Fast accompaniment:
**Tossed salad with lettuce, tomatoes, green onions,
black olives, cucumbers, and bottled dressing
Tube biscuits or crescent rolls**

Minestrone

Put in Crock-Pot:

1 cup dried kidney beans
2 cubes beef boullion
1 clove garlic, chopped
3 celery stalks, chopped
1 16-ounce can tomatoes

6 cups water
1 onion, chopped
3 carrots, diced
2 tablespoons olive oil
pepper to taste

Cook on low all day. Add 1 cup cooked noodles before serving.

Chicken-and-Rice Casserole

2 cups cooked rice
2 cups cooked chicken
1 10¾-ounce can chunky chicken mushroom soup
1 ½ cups cheddar cheese, grated

Put rice in the bottom of a casserole dish. Cover with chicken and then spread soup over rice and chicken. Top with cheese and bake at 350° for 30 minutes.

How to make your family's mealtime great:

★ Turn off the ringer on the phone (don't forget to turn it back on later).

★ Turn off TV and radio during dinner; play only quiet background music.

★ Try to establish a regular dinnertime, which will have to be flexible, of course.

★ Encourage each person to say something about his or her day.

★ Keep it light and encourage laughter.

★ Involve kids in meal planning and preparation.

★ Try to stay at the table together for at least 30 minutes.

★ Try not to worry about how much or how little the children eat; keep it relaxed.

★ Try reading a brief family devotional thought.

★ If it's impossible for your family to have dinner together, aim for breakfast together.

★ Remember that even a few meals a week together are better than none.

Wholesome in a Hurry

For me, the hour before dinner is usually when the kids whine, the dog chews up a pillow, and telemarketers attack like a swarm of buzzing mosquitoes. Knowing what I'm going to prepare, or even having it partially done when that busy hour starts, takes at least part of the stress out of the atmosphere in my home.

If you can start making dinner in the morning:

Pork chops and gravy served with mashed potatoes

If you have about a half hour after work to fix dinner:

Easy sloppy joes served on buns

If you're desperate:

Lemon chicken

Fast accompaniment:

Cooked fresh spinach with butter

Pineapple rings with cottage cheese

Pork Chops and Gravy

6 pork chops
1 10 ¾-ounce can evaporated milk
1 10 ¾-ounce can cream of mushroom soup

Put pork chops into a Crock-Pot after trimming the fat.
Add evaporated milk and soup. Cook all day on low.

Easy Sloppy Joes

1 ½ pounds ground beef
1 bottle chili sauce
ketchup

Brown ground beef. Drain (I rinse it with hot water to remove fat). Add chili sauce and an equal amount of ketchup. Stir, heat through, and serve on buns.

Lemon Chicken

boneless, skinless chicken breasts
(as many as you need to feed your family)
Italian salad dressing
garlic powder

pepper
lemon juice

Brown chicken breasts in a frying pan with salad dressing. Season with pepper, garlic powder, and lemon juice. Cover and cook 10 minutes per side or until done.

> I passionately believe that the home dining table is our last remaining family gathering place. It's a place for friends and family to nourish the relationships that are at the heart of homes, neighborhoods, and communities.
> —GRAHAM KERR

Pleasing to Your Family's Palate

It's been a long day. My proposal at work was turned down this morning, and I'm determined to leave work-related thoughts at the door—the *other* side of the door. I won't bring them into the house with me. I want to be here with my children, not just in body, but in mind and spirit as well. I'm going to ask God to help me focus on what is important for this evening—these young ones he has entrusted to me. Mealtime memories will last a lot longer than that work project.

If you can start making dinner in the morning:
Sweet and sour chicken

If you have about a half hour after work to fix dinner:
Beef stroganoff

If you're desperate:
Breakfast for dinner—scrambled eggs, bacon or sausage, and toast

Fast accompaniment:
Sliced tomatoes

Sweet-and-Sour Chicken

4 chicken breast halves (boneless and skinless works fine too)
1 envelope onion soup mix
1 10-ounce jar apricot preserves
½ cup water
1 8-ounce bottle of Russian salad dressing

Put chicken breasts in Crock-Pot. Mix onion soup mix with apricot preserves and water. Pour over chicken. Cook on low all day. A half hour before serving, add Russian salad dressing and heat through. Serve over rice.

Beef Stroganoff

1½ pounds beef round steak
1 10¾-ounce can golden mushroom soup
1 cup sour cream
fresh mushrooms, chopped (optional)
1 tablespoon butter
1 large onion, chopped
1 bay leaf
salt and pepper

Cut round steak into bite-sized, boneless pieces with fat removed. Sauté with onion and butter. When brown, add soup, sour cream, mushrooms, if you wish, and the bay leaf. Season to taste. Simmer until the beef is tender. Serve over rice or noodles.

℘   ℘   ℘

Outstanding Standbys

One thing I'm pretty good at is compartmentalizing. By that I mean focusing on what I'm doing right then. When I'm at work, I bundle up my worries about finances, health, and other problems and place them carefully inside an imaginary carton. I close the top of the carton and put it over to one side of my mind. I open up my work carton, take out the materials I need to handle today, and give my full attention to my job.

That means when I am at home, I must package up my work concerns and set aside the work container until tomorrow when I am there. While some life issues struggle very hard to escape from their box and grab my attention at the wrong moments, and at times I'm tempted to lift the lid and just gaze in there for a few minutes, I find that by focusing on the "here and now," I do better work at whatever part of my life I'm handling right then.

Right now it's time to open the "dinner" box.

If you can start making dinner in the morning:
Tuna noodle casserole

If you have about a half hour after work to fix dinner:
**Hamburgers with or without special sauce,
served on buns**

If you're desperate:
Frozen or delivered pizza

Fast accompaniment:
**Combine sliced fresh cauliflower, broccoli,
and mushrooms with a
red-wine-vinegar-and-oil salad dressing**

Tuna Noodle Casserole

Put in Crock-Pot:

2 6-ounce cans tuna, drained
2 10 ¾-ounce cans cream of celery soup
1 10-ounce package frozen vegetables
10 ounces egg noodles, cooked and drained
2 tablespoons melted butter   2 tablespoons parsley flakes
½ cup toasted almonds, sliced   1 cup milk

Cook on low all day. Recipe may be halved easily.

Special Sauce for Hamburgers

2 tablespoons mayonnaise
1 tablespoon blue cheese
¼ cup chopped walnuts

Combine mayonnaise, blue cheese, and walnuts. (You might want to give your kids the option of substituting good old ketchup for this sauce.)

Whether, then, you eat or drink or whatever
you do, do all to the glory of God.
—1 Corinthians 10:31

Setting a Speed-and-Taste Record

One thing that made my mother a good cook was her willingness to work with whatever she had on hand. She told stories of when she and my dad were just starting out and the only things left in the kitchen for a few days before payday were cans of tuna and pork and beans, and that's what they had for dinner (no, that combination is not on today's menu).

When we were growing up, she would often use whatever fruit she had to make a great fruit salad. She'd use strawberries, bananas, grapes, berries, peach slices, cantaloupe balls, or orange sections, blend them all together and add some vanilla yogurt as a dressing. Or she would toss together the simple salad in today's accompaniment idea.

I think her willingness to experiment showed me how to concoct brave new foods when necessity demands.

If you can start making dinner in the morning:
Chicken tortillas

If you have about a half hour after work to fix dinner:
Broccoli cheese soup served with French bread

If you're desperate:
Roast beef and Swiss cheese sandwiches with lettuce, tomato, and honey mustard (optional) on Focaccia bread

Fast accompaniment:
Salad made of grated carrots, chopped apple with skin on, raisins, and mayonnaise, all mixed together

Chicken Tortillas

Mix together:

round, medium-sized tortillas
3 cups cooked chicken
1 10¾-ounce can cream of chicken soup
½ of a 15-ounce can tomatoes
2 tablespoons quick-cooking tapioca
½ of a 6-ounce can chilies

Line the bottom of Crock-Pot with tortillas. Add ⅓ of chicken mixture, sprinkle with chopped onion and grated cheddar cheese. Repeat layers. Cover and cook all day on low.

Broccoli-Cheese Soup

1 10-ounce package frozen broccoli
3 tablespoons butter
1 cup cheddar cheese, grated
salt and pepper
3 tablespoons flour
4 cups milk

Cook broccoli according to package directions. In another pan melt butter, add flour, and stir until smooth. Cook a few minutes, and add milk a little at a time, stirring until smooth and thickened. Add cheddar and then salt and pepper to taste. Cook over low heat until cheese is melted. Add broccoli and heat.

Do-It-Yourself Dinner

Ever since they were small, my children have enjoyed helping prepare food. I have photos of the three of them standing on kitchen chairs on the other side of my kitchen island, waiting eagerly to stir in an ingredient or roll out cookie dough.

Today's meal is a kid-pleaser because you can involve them in the preparation and serving process. They can stir the noodles into the cheese mixture if you're having macaroni and cheese or put together their own taco. Even small children can do more than we think they can, if we're willing to overlook some pretty hefty messes.

If you can start making dinner in the morning:
Split pea soup

If you have about a half hour after work to fix dinner:
Tacos

If you're desperate:
Family size box (or two) of macaroni and cheese

Fast accompaniment:
**Leaf lettuce, two chopped Granny Smith apples,
one cup salted cashews, grated Swiss cheese,
poppy seed or your favorite dressing**

Split Pea Soup

2 cups dried split peas
1 ham bone
1 cup onion, chopped

8 cups water
1 cup celery, chopped

Soak split peas in water overnight. Drain. In the morning put peas, water, ham bone, onion, and celery in Crock-Pot. Cook on low all day. Freeze some for later.

Tacos

ground beef
1 envelope taco seasoning
tomatoes
onion
1 can refried beans

taco shells
cheddar cheese
lettuce
1 jar salsa

Brown ground beef and add envelope of taco seasonings. Grate cheddar cheese (kids love to do this if they're big enough not to cut themselves on the grater). Chop tomatoes, lettuce, and onion, and put each in an individual bowl, along with a bowl of salsa. Put the contents of a can of refried beans in a bowl and warm in microwave. Warm hard or soft taco shells in microwave. Everyone assembles his own tacos.

More ways to get the kids involved in mealtime:

★ Give kids some creative opportunities. Andrew likes to cut flowers in the yard and arrange them, although he's stingy—he prefers to let them keep growing outside.

★ Give the red You Are Special plate to someone in the family once a week for getting a good grade, winning a soccer game, or helping a younger child.

★ Let the children arrange fruit or vegetables on a platter or add and stir ingredients for you.

★ Young kids can shuck corn and enjoy it, preferably outside over newspapers because of the mess.

★ They can grind a pepper mill over a dish.

★ Teach them to set the table.

Old Faithful Fare

Chili is one of those foods that says "warm and wonderful" to me. It reminds me of a chilly fall evening after you get home from a high school football game. There are more ways to make chili than there are spoken dialects in the world (not really), and one of my friends makes "chili" with cut-up chicken and cooked navy beans. Her chili is white! One of the best things about chili is that you can make a big pot and freeze portions to provide meals for busy days in the future.

If you can start making dinner in the morning:
Chili

If you have about a half hour after work to fix dinner:

Meatloaf

If you're desperate:

Leftovers—Microwave frozen homemade soup you saved

Fast accompaniment:

Chopped fresh onions, grated cheddar,
sour cream, and nacho chips
Tossed salad

Chili

2 pounds mild Italian sausage (casing removed), crumbled
2 pounds lean ground beef
3 15-ounce cans kidney beans   3 bell peppers, chopped
2 16-ounce cans diced tomatoes   2 onions, chopped
4 tablespoons chili powder   pepper
1 15-ounce can hot-and-spicy kidney beans   garlic powder

Cook sausage and beef until brown, drain off grease. Put into Crock-Pot the drained meat, bell peppers, onion, kidney beans, tomatoes, chili powder, and add garlic powder and black pepper to taste. Freeze some for leftovers.

Meatloaf

2 pounds ground beef
¼ cup Parmesan cheese
1 envelope onion soup mix
garlic powder
½ cup ketchup or 1 16-ounce can tomatoes

1 egg
½ onion, chopped
½ cup dried bread crumbs
pepper

Mix ground beef with egg, onion soup mix, bread crumbs, ketchup or tomatoes, Parmesan cheese, onion, and add garlic powder and pepper to taste. Shape into a loaf and place in a 9 x 13 baking dish. Bake 30 minutes at 375°.

Someone once said that the trouble with life is that it's so *daily*. That's how it is with meals too. They just keep happening, again and again, every day. Families need to eat regularly! You can give your family the great gift of a peaceful meal, no matter what you're serving, if you rely on God's strength, for those *daily* events, like meals.

He gives power to those who are tired and worn out; he offers strength to the weak.
—Isaiah 40:29 NLT

Scrumptious Supper

Remember my friend Carla, the one with the brown bags of papers stuffed in her closet and the burned-up microwave? I've learned many things from Carla, including how you can have faith even when your husband's business venture is going broke and you have two children in college.

I also learned about one of today's meal ideas from her. When my daughter was born, Carla brought me a big pan of Chicken Breasts Supreme, and since then I have taken it to several families who had a newborn or a sick family member. This dish is elegant, delicious, and simple to make. And every child I've ever served it to wanted to lick her plate clean.

If you can start making dinner in the morning:
Chicken breasts supreme

If you have about a half hour after work to fix dinner:
Yummy casserole

If you're desperate:
Tuna melts

Fast accompaniment:
Sliced red, green, or yellow peppers (or a combination of these) with Italian salad dressing
Cooked rice

Chicken Breasts Supreme

6 boneless, skinless breast halves   ¼ cup melted butter
1 10 ¾-ounce can cream of mushroom soup
1 6-ounce can mushroom stems and pieces
1 cup sour cream
salt and pepper

Put chicken in baking dish. Mix together melted butter, soup, mushroom stems and pieces, and sour cream. Season with salt and pepper. Spoon sauce over chicken and refrigerate. Bake for one hour at 350° when you get home.

Yummy Casserole

1 6-ounce can tuna or chicken
1 10 ¾-ounce can chicken-and-rice soup
1 10 ¾-ounce can cream of mushroom soup
½ of a 10-ounce can evaporated milk
2 cups chow mein noodles

Mix in a 9 x 13 baking pan tuna or chicken, soups, evaporated milk, and chow mein noodles. Bake at 375° for 35 minutes.

Tuna Melts

English muffin halves

tuna

onion, chopped (if desired)

mayonnaise

cheddar cheese, grated

Toast English muffin halves. Mix tuna with mayonnaise to taste, adding onion if desired. Place tuna mixture on English muffin and top with grated cheddar. Broil or microwave until cheese melts.

The preparation of good food is merely another expression of art, one of the joys of civilized living.
—DIONE LUCAS

On Your Mark, Get Set, Eat!

Moms know the difference between a speed eater and a snail eater because I think we all have at least one of each. Speedy downs his food in seconds and wants to race off and play. It's a challenge to get him to sit still while the rest of the family finishes eating. And Pokey is still at the table after everyone else is finished, wanting to finish her vegetables so she, too, can have dessert.

I started out with a goal of having our family sit at the table together for 30 minutes each evening, uninterrupted by the phone, which could ring and ring unanswered for all I cared. By the time my kids were teens, we were lucky to have 30 minutes a week together at the table, and to them, each incoming phone call was a matter of life or death that could not possibly be ignored.

What I've learned during this progression is that the pace of eating is not important, and even the food is not all that important. What matters is the connection—interrupted by the phone or not—that we gain from sharing meals.

No matter what happens during your dinnertime tonight, enjoy. It doesn't have to be perfect to be priceless time together.

If you can start making dinner in the morning:
Vegetable soup

If you have about a half hour after work to fix dinner:
Chicken and stuffing

If you're desperate:
French toast

Fast accompaniment:
Garlic bread
Sliced fresh fruit

Vegetable Soup

Put into Crock-Pot:

1 10-ounce package frozen green beans
1 32-ounce can mixed vegetable juice
4 fresh or frozen tomatoes
1 envelope onion soup mix
½ head of cabbage
1 large red onion, sliced

Cook on low all day.

Chicken and Stuffing

6 thawed, bone-in chicken breasts
1 box stuffing mix

Bake chicken breasts at 375° for 30 minutes. Meanwhile, mix up a box of stuffing mix. When chicken is cooked, spread stuffing on top and serve.

French Toast

Stale or day-old bread slices
1 cup skim milk
1 egg

Dip bread slices in a mixture of milk and egg. Cook in a buttered skillet and serve with syrup or honey.

Garlic Bread

1 loaf sourdough bread
1 tablespoon olive oil
¼ cup Parmesan cheese

¼ cup melted butter
1 teaspoon garlic powder

Slice bread either lengthwise or across in round disks. Place on cookie sheet and heat oven to broil. Mix together melted butter, olive oil, garlic powder, and Parmesan cheese, and then spread on bread pieces. Broil until brown and bubbly.

> People should eat and drink and enjoy the fruits of their labor for these are gifts from God.
> —Ecclesiastes 3:13 NLT

Hassle-Free Home Cooking

One way to really save time on cooking dinner is to only cook every other day. Yes, that's right, don't cook every night. With a little planning, you can make large portions of several meals, freeze half, and pull them out to warm up on nights you're not cooking. Just be sure to stagger them so you don't hear a lot of whining about, "Not *that* again, Mom."

Some of my favorites to double up are sloppy joes, spaghetti sauce to be used multiple ways, cooked chicken, and soups and stews.

If you can start making dinner in the morning:
Turkey breast in Crock-Pot

If you have about a half hour after work to fix dinner:
Stuffed peppers

If you're desperate:
Fresh fish

Fast accompaniment:
**Fresh broccoli florets microwaved in a covered dish
with butter and small amount of water
Real or boxed mashed potatoes**

**Uses for frozen tomatoes from the garden
(or anywhere else):**

- ⭐ Spaghetti sauce
- ⭐ Chili
- ⭐ Soups
- ⭐ Lasagne sauce
- ⭐ Sloppy joes
- ⭐ Meatloaf addition
- ⭐ Stuffed peppers

Turkey Breast in Crock-Pot

Put in Crock-Pot:

1 thawed turkey breast
2 cups celery, chopped
2 cups onions, chopped

Cook all day on low. (Always a person who has to learn the hard way, I tried putting a frozen turkey breast in my Crock-Pot, and the insert cracked during cooking.)

Stuffed Peppers

6 bell peppers
⅓ cup chopped onion
½ cup cheddar cheese, grated
1 16-ounce can tomatoes, drained
1 teaspoon Worcestershire sauce
salt and pepper

1 pound ground beef
½ cup water
½ cup uncooked rice

Cut tops off of peppers and remove seeds and insides. Boil for about three minutes and drain. Cook ground beef with onion. Drain and add tomatoes, water, rice, and Worcestershire, and salt and pepper to taste. Cover and simmer until rice is tender (about 15 minutes). Add cheese. Stuff peppers and bake uncovered at 350° for 20 minutes.

Fresh Fish

salmon, cod, orange roughy, or your favorite fish

olive oil

fresh lemon juice

¼ cup water

Sauce

½ cup mayonnaise

1 tablespoon sweet pickle relish

¼ cup chili sauce

Cook fish in a small amount of olive oil. Add water. Cover and steam for a few minutes until done. (If fish was frozen, cook longer until meat is light-colored all the way through, adding water as necessary to keep from burning.) Season to taste and squeeze fresh lemon juice over. For a delicious sauce, combine mayonnaise, chili sauce, and sweet pickle relish.

❀   ❀   ❀

Uses for stale bread:

★ French toast

★ Bread pudding

★ Stuffing

★ Bread crumbs

★ Croutons

★ Bird feeder filler

Ready in Record Time

My sons ask for my biscuits for every holiday meal. Not only do they ask for them, but they ask me to make a quadruple batch! And that's a lot of biscuits. We stretch them out, though, keeping quite a few to go with leftovers for meals after the holiday. Microwaved for about ten seconds, the leftover biscuits are delicious to go with a dinner meal or with honey for breakfast.

If you can start making dinner in the morning:
Polish sausage and sauerkraut in Crock-Pot

If you have about a half hour after work to fix dinner:
Chicken Parmesan

If you're desperate:
Leftover casserole

Fast accompaniment:
Quick biscuits or crescent rolls
Mixed melon balls or slices
(cantaloupe, honeydew, and watermelon if in season)

Polish Sausage and Sauerkraut in Crock-Pot

Polish sausage
1 can or bag of sauerkraut (amount depending on how much your family will eat)

Slice sausage into ½-inch slices. Put into Crock-Pot with sauerkraut. Cook on low all day. This is a good recipe to make a lot of so you'll have leftovers.

Chicken Parmesan

½ cup Italian salad dressing
fine seasoned bread crumbs
boneless chicken breasts or strips
Parmesan cheese

Pour Italian salad dressing in one bowl. In a second bowl mix bread crumbs with an equal amount of cheese. Dip chicken breasts or strips in salad dressing and then in crumb mixture and bake in a greased pan at 350° for 35 minutes.

Quick (and Superb) Biscuits

2 cups flour
2 teaspoons baking powder
melted butter
pinch of salt
whipping cream

Put flour in a bowl and then add salt and baking powder. Mix in enough whipping cream (unwhipped) to create a sticky dough. Turn dough out onto a pastry cloth or board dusted with flour and knead it until it is smooth. Roll the dough into a rectangle, cut into square chunks, and dip chunks into melted butter before baking at 425° for 10 minutes.

> When it comes to cooking, five years ago I felt guilty "just adding water." Now I want to bang the tube against the countertop and have a five-course meal pop out. If it comes with plastic silverware and a plate that self-destructs, all the better.
> —ERMA BOMBECK

Simply Soup

When my sister and I were girls, we loved tomato soup because we thought wadded up white bread balls were especially delicious when soaked in the soup. I never could interest my children in our "dumplings," but they do like saltines crunched up in the soup, and I have even seen them dipping a grilled cheese sandwich in it.

If you can start making dinner in the morning:
Bean soup
Frozen fruit salad

If you have about a half hour after work to fix dinner:
Vegetable soup (leftover) with chicken and rice

If you're desperate:
Grilled cheese sandwiches and canned tomato soup

Fast accompaniment:
Cut up any kind of fruit you have and mix with vanilla yogurt

Bean Soup

1 12-ounce package dry bean soup
1 12-ounce can tomatoes and green chilies
2 cups cooked ham, cubed   1 onion, chopped
2 cloves garlic, minced   1 16-ounce can tomatoes
water

Pour beans into Crock-Pot and add water according to package directions. Add ham, onion, garlic, tomatoes, and tomatoes and green chilies. Cook all day on low.

Frozen Fruit Salad

8 ounces cream cheese
1 can fruit cocktail, drained   ¼ cup mayonnaise
2 cups miniature marshmallows   2 bananas, sliced
1 large container of whipped topping

Blend together cream cheese and mayonnaise and then add fruit cocktail, miniature marshmallows, and bananas. Fold in a large container of whipped topping. Freeze in a mold. Thaw 10 minutes before serving.

Chicken and Rice

boneless, skinless chicken breasts
olive oil spray

Sauté chicken breasts in olive oil spray. Cook any kind of rice you like. Chop chicken and add both to leftover soup.

Chicken time-saver: Always cook extra chicken breasts, cut up what you don't need, and freeze for use in another recipe on another day.

Disguise and Conquer

One little guy who ate lunch at our house when my children were small persistently refused to eat vegetables or fruit, sticking with a grilled cheese sandwich and chips.

"How about an apple, Rob?" I offered.

"No, thank you. I don't eat apples."

"Well, we have cucumbers too."

"No, thank you. I don't eat cucumbers."

"I'm sure your mom makes you eat fruits and vegetables. Which ones do you like?"

"I don't really like them at all."

Wanting to make the point to my own children that all kids and adults have to eat fruits and vegetables, I pursued the subject. "What vegetables do you eat at home for dinner then? Carrots, beans, broccoli, corn?"

"I don't eat real vegetables. I take vegetables and fruits in pills so I don't have to eat 'em."

I know his mother well enough to suspect that Rob does indeed have to eat "real vegetables," but I decided to let the issue go and get out dessert. It was vanilla yogurt with sliced strawberries and bananas in it, and I guess the yogurt disguised the fruit well enough because Rob ate a bowlful and asked for seconds.

If you can start making dinner in the morning:
Oven brunch dish

If you have about a half hour after work to fix dinner:
Salmon croquettes
(If you can get the kids to try them,
they'll like them. Maybe calling them
Pink Tuna Burgers would help.)

If you're desperate:
Chili tortillas
(You need leftover or frozen chili for this.)

Fast accompaniment:
Sliced fresh strawberries
combined with sliced bananas

Oven Brunch Dish

There are many variations on this, but my favorite is this one.

8 slices bread, diced

2 cups cheddar cheese, grated

1 10 ¾-ounce can cream of mushroom soup

1 teaspoon spicy mustard

1 pound cooked sausage, drained

1 small can of sliced mushrooms, drained

1 dozen eggs

1⅔ cups milk

Layer into greased 9 x 13 pan the diced bread mixed with the cheese, mushrooms, and sausage. Mix together eggs, soup, milk, and mustard, and pour mixture over bread-and-sausage layer. Assemble in the morning, refrigerate, and bake at 375° for 40 minutes right before dinnertime.

Salmon Croquettes

1 can salmon

½ cup bell pepper, chopped

1 cup saltine crackers, crushed

½ cup onion, chopped

1 egg

olive oil

Take all the icky stuff out of the salmon (bones, skin, and so on). Mix the salmon with onion, bell pepper, egg, and crackers. Form into patties and sauté in olive oil until brown on both sides.

Chili Tortillas

leftover chili
canned corn
tortillas

cheddar cheese, grated
canned tomatoes

Thaw frozen leftover chili in the microwave. Wrap about a half-cup of chili with a handful of shredded cheese and 1 tablespoon each canned corn and chopped tomatoes in a tortilla. Heat in microwave 1 minute or until heated through.

Keep fresh, washed fruit on a low refrigerator shelf or in an unbreakable bowl on the kitchen table so even a young child can help himself and get that grown-up feeling of choosing whether he wants a pear or an apple.

Birthday Cakes

It was the year my daughter, Carolyn, cut off her hair above the ear on only one side while she was playing Samson and Delilah (by herself) at age four. Those little kids' scissors *do* cut hair. After an emergency trip to a hair stylist, it turned out to be one of the cutest haircuts she ever had.

It was also the year her friend Michelle lost her shoe in our basement at Carolyn's birthday party and had to go home with only one. I found it several days later inside the little trampoline the girls had jumped on.

But my point here is birthday cakes. I used to make some adorable and inexpensive cakes for my children by buying cake pans shaped like bears or dogs or Ninja Turtles or Barbies at a discount restaurant supply store, and then making the cakes with the children's help.

I always made them from scratch because my mother always did that, but the children consistently expressed a preference for cake mixes, bottled spaghetti sauce, and other nonhomemade foods.

One of the best (and cheapest) cakes I used to make for my sons was the train cake. I baked a cake in a 9 x 13 cake pan, cooled it, and cut it into little train car rectangles, which we arranged on a cutting board covered with waxed paper, and then frosted. We put on little wheels made out of Skittles or other candies and a smokestack on the engine that was a piece of a licorice stick. It was a favorite with both boys. They loved decorating the cakes together and took extra pride in telling their friends they had helped.

If you can start making dinner in the morning:
Italian beef

If you have about a half hour after work to fix dinner:
Fun-filled burgers

If you're desperate:
Quick chicken fajitas

Fast accompaniment:

Canned pears or peaches with cottage cheese
Birthday cake

Italian Beef

Put into Crock-Pot:

1 2-pound beef roast
1 12-ounce jar of pepperoncinis (small, semi-hot peppers)
including the juice
1 bottle Italian salad dressing (optional)

Cook all day on low. Pull apart and serve on French bread. A slight flavor variation occurs if you add a bottle of Italian salad dressing as well.

Fun-Filled Burgers

1 pound hamburger
stuffed green olives, chopped   ketchup
1 cup cheddar cheese, grated

Make thin patties out of hamburger and divide into two groups. Spread about 2 tablespoons of a mixture of ketchup, stuffed green olives, and cheese on half the patties. Place another patty on top of each and pinch edges together. Sauté slowly in pan on stove and spoon sauce that comes from cooking over the burgers.

Quick Chicken Fajitas

10 chicken strips
garlic cloves, whole or minced
1 tablespoon olive oil
pepper
½ lemon or orange
soft taco shells

onion, chopped
bell peppers, chopped
cumin
fajita seasoning
1 bottle teriyaki sauce

Put chicken strips in a skillet. Add onion, garlic, peppers, and olive oil. Season with cumin, pepper, fajita seasoning, and orange or lemon juice squeezed over. Add teriyaki sauce if desired. Cook until chicken is done, stirring frequently. Wrap in warmed soft taco shells.

> Life's riches other rooms adorn,
> But in a kitchen home is born.
> —*Betty Crocker Picture Cookbook,* 1956

Green Is Yucky

When my kids were young, I had a reputation as the mom who would make all visiting kids eat weird stuff, like tomatoes and green peppers. The way I saw it, I couldn't very well insist that my own children eat their vegetables and let their friends get by without eating any. Except for little Rob, whose vitamins seemed to cover all of his nutritional bases, all the other children who visited us choked down at least a few bites of all that red, yellow, and green food I made them eat.

Now that they're all teenagers, I still have the reputation of having given them a good start on vegetable eating. I saw Brent's mother recently—he was a frequent visitor at our table—and she said six-foot-tall Brent credits *me* with his fondness for green peppers. Ah, vindicated at last.

If you can start making dinner in the morning:
Beef stew in Crock-Pot

If you have about a half hour after work to fix dinner:
Do-it-yourself baked potatoes

If you're desperate:
Veggie burgers (from frozen pack) served on buns

Fast accompaniment:
**Fresh green beans boiled in salt water with salt pork
or ham bone until tender-crisp**

Beef Stew in Crock-Pot

1 pound beef stew meat
2 tablespoons olive oil
pepper
1 8-ounce can of tomato sauce
2 medium onions, sliced
2 tablespoons ketchup
garlic powder

Combine stew meat, tomato sauce, 1 of the sliced onions, 1 tablespoon olive oil, pepper, garlic powder, and other seasonings you like. Cook on low all day. Sauté another medium sliced onion in the remaining olive oil, add ketchup, and stir into stew. Serve over rice.

Do-It-Yourself Baked Potatoes

baking potatoes

cheddar cheese, grated

sour cream (or plain yogurt)

leftover chicken, chopped

leftover vegetables (broccoli or squash, cooked; green onions or bell peppers, chopped)

chopped tomatoes

salsa

leftover chili

Microwave potatoes, about 8–10 minutes for two potatoes at once. Set out bowls of tomatoes, cheddar, sour cream or plain yogurt, salsa, vegetables, chicken, and chili. Everyone assembles her own potato.

Busy Hands

Even though one of today's recipes includes another kind of olives, a favorite activity for my kids during dinner preparation time was sticking a pitted black olive on each of their fingers and then eating them off one by one. I have several pictures of my children holding up olive-clad fingers. Whenever I was planning to use black olives in a salad, I would buy a can or two extra for them to play with. They never liked the green ones as much, but two out of my three love my mother's potato salad, which includes sliced stuffed green olives.

If you can start making dinner in the morning:
Olive chicken

If you have about a half hour after work to fix dinner:
Chicken stir-fry

If you're desperate:
Meatball soup

Fast accompaniment:
Baby carrots with ranch dressing

Olive Chicken

Put into Crock-Pot:

4 bone-in or boneless chicken breasts
1 6-ounce can tomato paste
1 small jar sliced stuffed green olives
salt and pepper, to taste
garlic powder, to taste

Cook on low all day. Serve over noodles.

Chicken Stir-Fry

3 boneless, skinless chicken breasts (fresh or frozen)
1 teaspoon olive oil
½ bottle stir-fry sauce
1 cup frozen sliced carrots
1 clove garlic, chopped
1 cup frozen sugar snap peas
2 cups cooked rice

Cut chicken breasts into strips and cook in olive oil with garlic about 5 minutes (longer if frozen) until chicken is cooked. Add stir-fry sauce, sugar snap peas, carrots, and cook until crisp. Stir in rice.

Meatball Soup

1 pound ground beef
1 cup peppers, chopped
1 envelope onion soup mix
2 cups cooked rice (optional)
1 cup onions, chopped
1 large can tomato juice
½ cup Parmesan cheese

Pinch ground beef into 1-inch balls. Brown in a Dutch oven. Drain and rinse meat. Add onions and peppers and cook until veggies are tender. Add tomato juice, onion soup mix, and cheese. Heat through. You may want to add the cooked rice when you serve the soup as a leftover.

My children never quite got the hang of milk toast. I made it for them many times, but somehow it wasn't the cure-all it had been for my sister, two brothers, and me. My children ate a couple of bites, but they never slurped it down and asked for more the way we did when we were kids.

If you can start making dinner in the morning:
Garlic-stuffed pork roast

If you have about a half hour after work to fix dinner:
Turkey or chicken divan

If you're desperate:
Frozen breaded chicken tenders
Milk toast

Fast accompaniment:
Applesauce

Garlic-Stuffed Pork Roast

pork roast
6 cloves garlic
2 tablespoons water

Make slits in a pork roast from which fat has been trimmed. Insert whole garlic cloves. Put into Crock-Pot with the water. Cook on low all day.

Keeping foods fresher:

If you store these items in the freezer, they'll stay fresher and last longer, especially if you can store them in their original unopened containers:

* ✿ coffee
* ✿ nuts
* ✿ unpopped popcorn
* ✿ marshmallows
* ✿ potato chips
* ✿ pretzels
* ✿ crackers

Milk Toast

When I was a child, my mother made us "milk toast" whenever we were sick. I recently observed the mother of a friend fixing the same thing for her grandchild and calling it "buttery broth," and in *Angela's Ashes*, Frank McCourt's mother called it "bread and goody." You toast two pieces of bread, simultaneously warming up some milk in the microwave, or in my mother's case, on the stove in a pan. Generously butter both slices of the toast and sprinkle a good amount of sugar on each one as you place them in a bowl. Pour hot milk over it all, and boy, is that stuff delicious. And, at least for me, it really does have medicinal properties. I still fix it for myself on occasion if I feel like I'm coming down with something. Maybe it's a placebo, but I feel warmed and better after a good batch of milk toast.

Turkey or Chicken Divan

3 cups cooked, cubed turkey or chicken
2 packages frozen broccoli, cooked
6 slices American cheese, diced   1 can evaporated milk
1 can French-fried onions
1 can mushroom soup

Layer in a 9 x 13 pan the chicken, broccoli, and cheese. Mix together the evaporated milk and soup and spread it over. Bake at 375° for 25 minutes. Sprinkle on a can of French fried onions and heat through.

Ways to add calcium to your diet:

1. Add skim milk to your coffee (I put in a dollop of honey too).

2. Stir-fry a cup or two of dark green vegetables, like spinach, kale, or mustard greens, and add toasted sliced or slivered almonds.

3. Toast sprouted grain bread.

4. Enjoy a glass of chocolate milk with your kids.

5. Prepare Jell-O pudding using milk.

6. Add low-fat cheese to eggs or omelettes.

7. Have a bean burrito in a corn tortilla for lunch.

Tradition

A friend of my mother told me this joke: A wife cut off the two ends of a pot roast before she put it in the pan to bake. Her husband, noticing this, remembered that his mother hadn't done it that way, so he asked his wife why she cut the ends off first.

"It's the way Mother always did it," she replied. "I don't really know why it's done this way."

When they visited the mother-in-law at Christmas, the husband asked her why she did it that way.

"It's just the way my mother always did it," she said.

The next summer at a family reunion, he asked the grandmother the same question.

She laughed. "The only reason I did that was that I only had a small pan and had to cut the ends off the roast to fit it in my pan."

So there was no reason for this method of pot roast preparation to be carried on down through the generations, but it was anyway.

Traditions are great, but sometimes we need to ask ourselves why we do something a certain way. Taking a fresh look at the way you do things can unleash your creativity and lead to an even better way of doing it.

If you can start making dinner in the morning:
Roast beef without ends cut off in Crock-Pot

If you have about a half hour after work to fix dinner:
Frozen salmon fillet

If you're desperate:

Turkey burgers (just like beef hamburgers but made with ground turkey)

Fast accompaniment:

Baked potatoes cooked in microwave served with salsa instead of butter or sour cream

Roast Beef in Crock-Pot

1 sirloin tip roast
1 envelope onion soup mix
1 10¾-ounce can cream of mushroom soup

Put roast in Crock-Pot. Add onion soup mix and cream of mushroom soup. Cook on low all day. (Cook a large roast so you can freeze some for later.)

Salmon Fillet

frozen salmon fillet
2 tablespoons teriyaki sauce   pepper
1 tablespoon water   lemon juice

Place salmon fillet in a skillet. Season it with pepper, lemon juice, and teriyaki sauce. Add water. Cover and cook until light pink all the way through.

Clucking Along

Is there any food more versatile than chicken? Okay, I guess you could say bread, milk, cheese, or eggs might be more versatile, but chicken is my favorite because it's healthy and it can be prepared so many ways, usually quickly and inexpensively.

I could (and often do) eat chicken day in and day out. I love chicken Caesar salads at restaurants or chicken fajitas with guacamole. And at home I can usually whip up a chicken dish with almost no preparation, even if all I have is frozen chicken breasts or strips.

So today I want to say "hats off!" to those wonderful hens that make it all possible.

If you can start making dinner in the morning:
Chicken paprika

If you have about a half hour after work to fix dinner:
Delicious chicken salad (thaw some frozen cooked and cubed chicken in the morning)

If you're desperate:
Turkey, spinach, and tomato sandwich with mayonnaise or spicy mustard

Fast accompaniment:
Quick fruit salad (combine grapes, bananas, berries, melon, or whatever you have on hand and blend in 1 can peach pie filling)

Chicken Paprika

Put in Crock-Pot:

2 medium onions, sliced
2 tablespoons olive oil
½ teaspoon salt
½ teaspoon garlic powder
1 16-ounce can stewed tomatoes
4 boneless, skinless chicken breasts, sliced

1 bell pepper, chopped
3 tablespoons paprika
½ teaspoon pepper
¼ cup sour cream

Cook on low all day and serve over buttered noodles.

Delicious Chicken Salad

4 cups cooked chicken
½ teaspoon salt
¾ cup mayonnaise
toasted almonds, sliced
lemon juice (optional)
curry powder (optional)

1 cup celery, chopped
¼ teaspoon pepper
¼ cup sour cream
1 cup seedless grapes
(any color), halved

Combine chicken with celery, grapes, salt, pepper, mayonnaise, and sour cream. Top with toasted almonds. Good warm or cold. Add a little curry powder and lemon juice if you like.

Sweet Tooth

When we were growing up, my sister loved sweets, especially chocolate. My mother even made chocolate pancakes for Sally, and in a supreme effort to get her to eat her vegetables, she once served her chocolate-covered peas, which became a great family joke thereafter. I think Sal would have especially enjoyed today's cranberry pork roast.

If you can start making dinner in the morning:
Cranberry pork roast

If you have about a half hour after work to fix dinner:
Salmon potato casserole

If you're desperate:
Frozen pie crust with liquid quiche mix, baked according to package directions

Fast accompaniment:
Fresh broccoli and cauliflower with curry dip (1 cup mayonnaise blended with 1 teaspoon curry powder (more if you like it stronger)

Cranberry Pork Roast

1 bag fresh cranberries
1 orange, sliced

1 to 2 pound pork roast
honey

Chop cranberries and put them in the bottom of Crock-Pot. Put in the pork roast. Cover it with orange slices and drizzle honey over it. Season with a dash each of cinnamon, cloves, salt, and pepper. Cook all day on low.

Salmon Potato Casserole

leftover potatoes, sliced

salt and pepper

¼ cup milk

1 10 ¾-ounce can cream of celery soup

1 small can of salmon

onion powder (or flakes)

potato chips, crushed

Layer potatoes and salmon in a buttered casserole dish. Season with salt, pepper, and onion powder or flakes. Mix soup with milk and pour over potatoes and salmon. Cover with crushed potato chips and bake for 30 minutes at 350°.

The Taste of Home

We had a grape arbor in our backyard when I was growing up, and some years my mother and her neighbor friends would spend several days making grape jelly. I've never made jelly since then except for a frozen strawberry variety one year, probably because I recall the process as being very involved. They would boil all the Ball jars, wash the grapes, cook them, melt wax to go over the top, and it seemed as though the house was torn up for quite a while as a result.

But, boy, was that grape jelly good. I wonder if just knowing all the work that went into it made it extra delicious. Today I have friends who give homemade grape, strawberry, or blueberry jam or jelly for Christmas gifts, and I look forward to receiving them from the Millers and other friends. There have been times when my jar of Christmas jam didn't even last until New Year's because my family practically sat down with the jar and a spoon and polished it off.

If you can start making dinner in the morning:
Chicken and noodles

If you have about a half hour after work to fix dinner:
Breakfast pizza—good for any meal

If you're desperate:
Jelly and cream cheese sandwiches

Fast accompaniment:
Grapefruit halves

Chicken and Noodles

1 whole chicken
celery, chopped
cumin
1 cup medium egg noodles
onions, chopped
pepper
garlic powder
1 cup water

Put the chicken into Crock-Pot. Add onions and celery, and then sprinkle with pepper, cumin, and garlic powder. Pour in water. Cook on low all day. Remove chicken and bone it. Meanwhile, put noodles into Crock-Pot liquid and cook for 30–45 minutes until noodles are tender.

Breakfast Pizza

1 pound pork sausage
1 package crescent rolls
1 cup hash browns, frozen and loose-pack
1 cup cheddar cheese, grated
5 eggs
¼ cup milk
2 tablespoons Parmesan cheese
salt and pepper

While browning sausage, flatten crescent rolls out on a pizza pan so that they cover it. Spread sausage on crust, and then sprinkle on hash browns and cheddar cheese. Beat together eggs, milk, and cheese, add salt and pepper to taste, and pour over crust. Bake at 375° for 25–30 minutes.

Enough for an Army

My mother made food in huge quantities. We always knew there would be plenty for friends if we brought anyone home after school. It seemed as though she made vats of spaghetti sauce or oyster stew for Christmas or potato salad in the summer. Unfortunately, sometimes we weren't able to use it all up before it had to be thrown away, and Mother's grocery bills were substantial.

When I established my own home, I found myself doing the same thing. I prepared food as if I were having company every day. Seeing the cost and the waste, I trimmed back to smaller quantities, only to have that backfire. One evening when my extended family was over for dinner, my brother John asked for more spaghetti sauce—and I had run out! The unthinkable had happened, and I never heard the end of it from my family, all of whom like to eat.

Today I try hard to strike the balance between having plenty for everyone and not having so much I wind up throwing part of it away, and it's not easy to do. I guess I'd still rather err on the side of plenty, just the way Mother always did.

If you can start making dinner in the morning:
Pork chop casserole

If you have about a half hour after work to fix dinner:
Grilled or sautéed steak or boneless chicken breast, seasoned to taste

If you're desperate:
Chicken or turkey bratwursts warmed in a skillet and served on buns

Fast accompaniment:
Fast fruit salad

Pork Chop Casserole

potatoes, peeled and sliced
onion, sliced
4 to 6 pork chops
1 10¾-ounce can tomato soup

Layer potatoes, onion, and pork chops in Crock-Pot. Pour in tomato soup. Cook on low all day.

Fast Fruit Salad

unpeeled apples
raisins
salt

mini marshmallows
sliced bananas
mayonnaise

Cut up apples, marshmallows, raisins, and bananas in equal proportions. Add a dash of salt and mix with mayonnaise to taste.

> **Relationship building:** Invite your extended family over once a month for a meal, pizza, or dessert. The cousins can become closer friends while adults enjoy one another's company as well.

Having Company, Texas Style

One year while my children were elementary school students, my friend Cynthia, an actress, artist, and superb cook, hosted the Texas Barbecue for all the school families. The event kicked off the preview of our big Country Stores craft sale that had been held for at least 35 years when we were part of the school family.

Cynthia brought in bales of hay and checkered tablecloths and giant bags of peanuts that we strewed all over the floor of the gym. She strung tiny white Christmas lights and lights in the shape of chili peppers all around the gym, and brought in horse saddles and other western memorabilia for decorations.

She even cooked all the barbecue beef and corn pudding herself, purchased all the bread, cole slaw, and pies for dessert, and we served about 300 people for dinner. It was an exhausting but rewarding event, and no one ever forgot the Texas Barbecue. One of today's main dishes reminds me of my dear friend Cynthia.

If you can start making dinner in the morning:
Barbecue beef

If you have about a half hour after work to fix dinner:

Peanut soup

If you're desperate:

Ham and cheese sandwiches

Fast accompaniment:

Coconut fruit salad

Corn on the cob

Barbecue Beef

Put in Crock-Pot:

Sirloin tip roast

1 jar barbecue sauce

Cook on low all day.

Peanut Soup

2 tablespoons butter

⅓ cup celery, chopped

¼ teaspoon salt

¾ cup chicken broth

crumbled crisp bacon

⅓ cup onion, chopped

1 tablespoon flour

2 cups milk

½ cup peanut butter

Melt butter in a pan. Add onion and celery and cook about 5 minutes. Blend in flour and salt and heat until bubbly. Add milk and chicken broth gradually, stirring until smooth. Bring to a boil. Carefully blend mixture into peanut butter in metal bowl. Return to pan and heat. Sprinkle bowls of soup with crumbled crisp bacon.

Coconut Fruit Salad

4 cups fresh, frozen, or canned fruit
1 cup sour cream
1 cup coconut

Mix fruit with sour cream and coconut and then chill.
Serve on lettuce.

ℐ℮ ℐ℮ ℐ℮

The Fun of Pretending

My son Steve, the youngest, loved to go down into our basement game room with me or anyone in the family who would play with him and embark on a game of "Be Anything and Do Anything." He had invented this game when he was about three years old, and I'd lie on the floor while he stacked blocks or pushed cars and trucks around the flat Berber carpeting. He'd say, "Mom, let's pretend that we can be anything and do anything," and then he'd proceed to construct imaginary buildings, road systems, or amusement parks using his sharp young mind and whatever toys were at hand.

This game developed into "Businessman," something I played with my children, nieces, and nephews. I gave each of the children a pad of yellow paper and a pen. We used an old phone with no cord, and each child was assigned a job. My nephew Paul would get on the phone and check references on all the employees we needed to hire. His brother Michael served as the architect for the project. The girls bargained for and purchased office furniture and other supplies. My son Andrew wrote up a list of all the supplies and materials we would need and costed them all out, and Steve thought up elaborate scenarios for our projects. We played this game for long periods, even when the kids reached their teens.

If you don't like today's menu, use that sharp imagination of yours and say, "Let's pretend I can cook anything or creatively recycle some leftovers today."

If you can start making dinner in the morning:
Corned beef and cabbage

If you have about a half hour after work to fix dinner:
Spicy chicken

If you're desperate:
Chicken wrap

Fast accompaniment:
Fresh fruit: sliced unpeeled apples, melon chunks, strawberries

Corned Beef and Cabbage

corned beef brisket
cabbage, sliced
garlic powder

2 cups water
pepper

Place corned beef brisket into Crock-Pot with water. Add a washed and sliced half or whole head of cabbage, season with pepper and garlic powder, cover, and cook all day on low.

Spicy Chicken

2 tablespoons Italian salad dressing
1 teaspoon garlic powder   ¼ cup spicy mustard
2 tablespoons water
4 boneless, skinless chicken breasts

Mix together Italian salad dressing, garlic powder, mustard, and water. Put in a plastic bag with chicken breasts cut into strips and shake to coat. Place in a greased 9 x 13 pan and bake at 375° for 30 minutes.

Chicken Wrap

Precooked chicken, chopped
onions, sliced   1 tablespoon olive oil
corn or flour tortillas   bell peppers, sliced
mayonnaise (optional)   mustard (optional)
cloves of garlic, whole and peeled (optional)

Sauté chicken in olive oil with onions and green peppers. Add garlic cloves if you have some. Warm corn or flour tortillas in microwave and fill with chicken mixture. Add mustard or mayonnaise if desired.

℘   ℘   ℘

It's a Party!

When my kids were little they loved to do what we called "Snack for Dinner." We would have something like the appetizers in today's recipes or sandwiches they made themselves with bowls of cut-up fresh fruit or even their favorite cereal.

In fact, they often asked if we couldn't "Snack for Dinner" even when I had a meal prepared. It was something out of the ordinary to them, and they considered it to be a special treat. Snacking for dinner was easy on me too, unless I had already prepared a regular dinner.

If you can start making dinner in the morning:
Peanut pork roast

If you have about a half hour after work to fix dinner:
**Appetizers for dinner—
mini sandwiches and nachos**

If you're desperate:
**Ham slice warmed in covered skillet with
2 tablespoons orange marmalade and
1 teaspoon water
or Snack for dinner**

Fast accompaniment:
**Sweet potatoes cooked in microwave
Tropical salad**

Peanut Pork Roast

1 to 2 pound pork roast
1 cup orange juice
½ cup peanut butter

Put pork roast in Crock-Pot. Add orange juice and peanut butter. Cook on low all day.

Mini Sandwiches

2 4½-ounce cans deviled ham
2 8-ounce packages cream cheese, softened
tiny rye bread slices
green olives

Mix deviled ham with cream cheese. Toast rye bread slices on a cookie sheet under the broiler. Spread mixture on toast and top with a green olive slice.

Nachos

canned refried beans
round nacho chips
cheddar cheese slices
jalapeno pepper slices

Spread refried beans (the kind with sausage are really good) on nacho chips. Top with cheddar cheese and a tiny bit of a jalapeno pepper. Broil until cheese melts.

Tropical Salad

1 cup orange chunks
3 tablespoons lemon juice
1 cup mayonnaise
¼ cup pitted dates, chopped
1 cup seedless green grapes

2 bananas, sliced
½ cup whipped cream
½ cup coconut

Combine orange chunks, bananas, grapes, dates, lemon juice, whipped cream, and mayonnaise. Top with coconut.

ℰ   ℰ   ℰ

No-Way Pizza

I'm going to admit that I cannot make homemade pizza. I've tried and no one has been willing to eat it. I've attempted various recipes, various crusts—homemade and store-bought—but my pizzas always turn out like a soggy checkerboard of vegetable and meat hunks swimming in runny sauce and blobs of melted cheese. I used to make little individual pizzas on English muffins that I thought were pretty good, but I've been begged not to make them again. So if you have a foolproof, failsafe homemade pizza recipe, I'd sure appreciate it if you would share it with me. And my family would too!

If you can start making dinner in the morning:
Round steak in Crock-Pot

If you have about a half hour after work to fix dinner:
Pizza burgers

If you're desperate:
Deviled eggs or egg salad sandwiches

Fast accompaniment:
**Fresh asparagus cooked in an inch of water
in a covered pan**

Round Steak in Crock-Pot

1 2-pound round steak
1 envelope onion soup mix
½ cup chopped celery
1 8-ounce can tomato sauce

salt and pepper
garlic powder
½ cup chopped onion

Put round steak in Crock-Pot. Season with salt, pepper, garlic powder, onion soup mix. Add celery, onion, and tomato sauce. Cook all day. Serve over rice or mashed potatoes.

Pizza Burgers

1 pound ground beef
3 tablespoons tomato paste
mozzarella cheese
2 tablespoons frozen or dried onion, chopped
2 tablespoons green olives, chopped

¼ cup Parmesan cheese
1 teaspoon oregano
hamburger buns

Mix beef with cheese, onions, olives, oregano, and tomato paste. Shape into burgers and cook in skillet. Melt mozzarella on burgers and serve on buns. Double for a larger (or hungrier) family.

Deviled Eggs

1 dozen eggs
salt and pepper
1 tablespoon spicy mustard
pickle relish (optional for egg salad)

⅓ cup mayonnaise
paprika

Hard boil eggs. Drain and let cool. Cut in half lengthwise, putting cooked and chopped yolks in a bowl. Add mayonnaise and mustard, and then salt and pepper to taste. Spoon into egg whites and sprinkle with paprika. If you're making egg salad, just chop the eggs and mix everything together. Adding pickle relish is good too.

A Sign of Summer

Our town features a French market every Saturday morning in the summer. It's an outside farm stand in our downtown area near the train station, and it's really fun to attend. My children like to walk through it with me and buy a warm bagel, a fresh melon, a basket of peaches, a jar of honey or real maple syrup, or a pot of annuals to add to our front porch. Farmers and other merchants come from miles around to set up every Saturday for half a day in the summer and fall, and the market is well attended.

I don't know how they do it, but the farmers' tomatoes and peppers come in much earlier than my little crop, so I love going over and getting the fresh produce every week before I'm able to harvest my own.

If it's summer and you can get homegrown tomatoes for today's BLTs, you're in for a treat. In the winter I buy the vine-ripened version, which tastes less cardboardy to me than others available at the grocery store.

If you can start making dinner in the morning:
Pepper steak

If you have about a half hour after work to fix dinner:
Ham kabobs

If you're desperate:
BLTs

Fast accompaniment:
Bean salad

Pepper Steak

Put in Crock-Pot:

1 pound round steak, in strips
¼ cup soy sauce
½ teaspoon ginger
1 cup onion, sliced
1 cup bell pepper, sliced
2 tomatoes, chopped

1 clove garlic, chopped
¼ cup olive oil
1 cup green onion, sliced
1 cup celery, sliced

Cook on low all day and serve over rice.

Ham Kabobs

ham chunks
cherry tomatoes
½ cup ketchup
2 teaspoons dry mustard

pineapple chunks
orange wedges
1 tablespoon olive oil

Thread ham chunks, pineapple chunks, cherry tomatoes, and orange wedges on skewers. Mix together ketchup, olive oil, and dry mustard and then brush on kabobs. Grill or broil.

Bacon, Lettuce, and Tomato Sandwiches

bacon (use turkey bacon, if you'd like)

bread

lettuce leaves

tomatoes, sliced

salt and pepper

mayonnaise

Cook bacon in microwave until crisp. Spread mayonnaise on bread and then layer bread, bacon, lettuce, and tomatoes. Sprinkle on salt and pepper before adding top layer of bread.

Bean Salad

1 15-ounce can green beans, drained

1 15-ounce can wax beans, drained

1 15-ounce can kidney beans, drained

½ cup bell pepper, chopped

Dressing:

¼ cup sugar

¼ cup olive oil

½ cup vinegar

salt and pepper

Combine equal size cans of green beans, wax beans, and kidney beans. Add bell pepper. For the dressing, mix together sugar, vinegar, and olive oil, and then salt and pepper to taste.

> It's difficult to think anything but
> pleasant thoughts while eating a
> homegrown tomato.
> —Lewis Grizzard

Mini-Farming

In the yard I inherited from my home's previous owners, many herbs grow, including mint, oregano, chives, basil, and lemon balm. My son Andrew loves to go out there and pick spices for use in a dish we're preparing.

My next-door neighbors had guests from Romania who spotted my big sorrel plant and asked if they could pick some to use in soup. It's a very fragrant type of celery with hollow stalks, and we've started drying and pulverizing it to add to dishes. The pulverizing part is especially fun for Andrew these days. He dries it in the microwave and mashes it in a wooden bowl so we can put it in soups and stews for added flavor.

We also grow tomatoes and green bell peppers, and every year I try growing spinach and lettuce, which the animals consume before the vegetables are big enough to pick. Last year we tried growing giant pumpkins; they grew lovely stems and flowers but were cut down overnight by some sort of worms, or so I've been told. This year we're going to try putting aluminum foil under all the stems as a preventative tactic.

A little fresh oregano would be delicious in any of today's dinners.

If you can start making dinner in the morning:
Italian chicken

If you have about a half hour after work to fix dinner:
Spaghetti and meatballs

If you're desperate:
Frozen ravioli boiled and served with bottled sauce

Fast accompaniment:
Italian eggplant

Italian Chicken

Put in Crock-Pot:
6 boneless, skinless chicken breasts (or a whole chicken)
1 tablespoon olive oil
1 onion, sliced
1 handful garlic cloves, peeled
1 16-ounce can tomatoes
1 bay leaf
oregano, to taste
pepper, to taste

Cook on low all day. Serve with noodles.

Spaghetti and Meatballs

1 cup bread crumbs (seasoned or plain)
1 pound ground beef   ¼ cup Parmesan cheese
1 egg (optional)   oregano
1 pound spaghetti, cooked   salt and pepper
1 jar spaghetti sauce

Combine bread crumbs, beef, cheese, and, if you like, an egg and then add oregano, salt, and pepper to taste. Form into balls and cook in hot olive oil until done. Add to homemade or bottled sauce and serve over spaghetti. You'll be a hero(ine).

Italian Eggplant

1 medium-sized eggplant
dry seasoned bread crumbs   melted butter
1 cup mozzarella cheese, grated   tomato sauce
    oregano

Peel and slice eggplant. Dip slices first in melted butter and then in dry seasoned bread crumbs. Put in a 9 x 13 pan and cover with tomato sauce. Sprinkle with oregano and cover with cheese. Bake at 450° for 10–12 minutes.

> **Spicy tip:** When using fresh herbs
> (like oregano and chives from the garden), use
> three times as much as you use when
> you use dried herbs.

An Occasional Splurge

When we used to vacation in Galena, Illinois, we loved to go to Emmy Lou's Café for breakfast. While what I'm about to admit was very unhealthy eating, for a special occasion my boys would order corned beef hash with poached eggs on top and banana cream pie for dessert! And their mother would order the same thing!

We tried to eat well for the most part, but if you tried Emmy Lou's corned beef hash and cream pies, you would understand why we had to make this wild exception from time to time.

If you can start making dinner in the morning:
Fruity pot roast

If you have about a half hour after work to fix dinner:
Ground beef casserole

If you're desperate:
**Canned corned beef hash served with ketchup.
Poached eggs on top are good, too.**

Fast accompaniment:
Fresh fruit, chopped and mixed

Fruity Pot Roast

Put in Crock-Pot:

1 3-pound beef roast
½ cup celery, chopped
2 cups mixed dried fruit
pepper, to taste

½ cup onion, chopped
½ cup carrots, chopped
garlic powder, to taste

Cook all day on low. Serve over rice or noodles.

Ground Beef Casserole

1 pound ground beef
1 cup cheddar cheese, grated
2 cups egg noodles, dry
½ cup fresh, frozen, or dried onions, chopped
6 ounces tomato paste (1 small can tomato sauce works well too)

garlic powder
pepper
1 16-ounce can tomatoes

Cook beef with onions. Drain. Cook the noodles. Stir into the beef-and-onion mixture the tomatoes, tomato paste (or tomato sauce), cooked noodles, cheese, and add pepper and garlic powder to taste. Bake in a casserole dish 30 minutes at 375°.

Health Food: Add garlic and onions (fresh, frozen, or minced garlic in a jar) to as many of your meals as you can, and use olive oil spray or a small amount of olive oil to sauté them in. Garlic and onions are good with:

    ✸ Grilled or sautéed chicken breasts

    ✸ Hamburgers and cheeseburgers

    ✸ Meatloaf

    ✸ Pork chops

    ✸ Buttered noodles

    ✸ Even scrambled eggs!

Something Pretty for Lunch

Did you know that pansies and nasturtiums are edible? Nasturtiums taste like radishes to me, and since they grow profusely from seeds every year, I harvest a healthy crop and put them in salads. My children think it's too weird to eat flowers, but they sure do make a salad look attractive— until they're picked out. I plant them at the base of my rosebushes, and the rose food seems to agree with the nasturtiums because I get enormous crops that I need to thin out so they don't overtake the roses.

If you can start making dinner in the morning:
Seasoned pork roast

If you have about a half hour after work to fix dinner:
Pork chops with Spanish rice

If you're desperate:

Dinner salad

Fast accompaniment:

Baked broccoli

Seasoned Pork Roast

Put in Crock-Pot:

pork roast
bell pepper, chopped
1 lemon, sliced

celery, chopped
onions, sliced
2 cups tomato juice

Cook on low all day. Serve with rice.

Pork Chops with Spanish Rice

6 pork chops
1 teaspoon chili powder
½ cup bell pepper, chopped
½ fresh or frozen onion, chopped
½ cup cheddar cheese, grated

pepper, to taste
¾ cup uncooked rice
2 16-ounce cans tomatoes

Brown pork chops in a skillet. Drain. Season with pepper and chili powder. Add rice, onion, and bell pepper. Pour tomatoes over all. Cover and cook 35 minutes, stirring occasionally. Top with cheese.

Dinner Salad

romaine lettuce
ham and/or turkey strips
chunks of cheese
2 hard-boiled eggs, sliced
tomato wedges

Break up washed romaine lettuce. Add ham and/or turkey strips, chunks of your favorite cheese, hard-boiled eggs, and tomato wedges. Toss in anything suitable from your garden and add croutons if you have them. Pass your favorite dressing.

Baked Broccoli

2 10-ounce packages frozen broccoli
1 10 ¾-ounce can cream of celery soup
1 small jar pimientos, chopped
4 ounces water chestnuts, sliced
½ cup milk
½ cup bread crumbs

Cook broccoli according to package directions. Drain. Mix cream of celery soup and milk and heat. Stir in pimientos and water chestnuts and then pour mixture over broccoli in a greased 9 x 13 pan. Sprinkle with bread crumbs. Bake 20 minutes at 375° or microwave for 3 minutes.

Ingredients to always have on hand

(check off in pencil to reuse list):

Item	Have X	Need X
White flour		
Whole wheat flour		
White sugar		
Brown sugar		
Powdered sugar		
Milk*		
Graham crackers		
Baking powder		
Baking soda		
Vanilla extract		
Semisweet chocolate chips		
Dry unsweetened cocoa		
Minced garlic		
Fresh or frozen onions and green peppers		
Bags of frozen vegetables		
Fresh or frozen bread		
Eggs		
Noodles in various shapes		
Rice		
Cheddar, mozzarella, and Parmesan cheese		
Peanut butter		
Jelly		
Tuna		
Canned soup		
Canned tomatoes, tomato paste, and tomato sauce		
Canned fruit your kids like		
Raisins		
Applesauce		
Mayonnaise		
Mustard		
Butter		
Olive oil		
Spices: whole peppercorns (if you have a pepper mill), garlic powder, cumin, oregano, mixed blend, fajita blend, curry powder, cinnamon, nutmeg		
Soy and teriyaki sauces		
Vinegar		
Ketchup		
Pancake syrup and honey		
Fresh fruits and vegetables		
Fresh or frozen meats, chicken, and fish		

* I like to keep buttermilk on hand for waffles and pancakes, but it's not a necessity. Powdered buttermilk is also available.

There's Nothing like a friend

Nurturing Your Relationships with God and Others

🍥 🍥 🍥

You may have heard about the thirsty boy who passed around his canteen to all of his equally thirsty friends, and by the time it returned to him it was empty, leaving his thirst unslaked. When another friend joined the group later and asked for a drink, the boy held his canteen upside down to demonstrate its emptiness. If he had refilled his canteen before it was empty, he would have had enough water for himself and also for the new boy. He wanted to share, but he had nothing left to give.

We moms also give and give to take care of the needs of others, often becoming depleted in the process. If we don't refill our spiritual and emotional tanks, we can burn out and respond to a need with a sigh or even a snarl instead of with the energy and love we want to give. If my canteen is empty, I have no refreshment to offer to others.

I grew up believing that thinking of myself was simply selfish. *Think of others, not yourself.* And certainly there's

125

value in the idea of focusing on others' needs and not just on your own. But what I've noticed is that those who pour themselves out for others—whether it be in ministry, motherhood, or career—without caring for their own needs as well eventually run out of energy with which to help others. I've come to the conclusion that self-care is really stewardship—taking care of one of the gifts that God has given to me: my life and my body. My physical, emotional, and spiritual health is important to God, and he expects me to give it a reasonable amount of care.

In this chapter you will find ways to refill your canteen with some brief activities you can squeeze into your busy life. The ideas are surprisingly simple, but also surprisingly effective in nurturing your spiritual and emotional health. They include spending time with God, spending time with other people, and laughing.

I trust that after you read this chapter, you will feel at least slightly more relaxed and will have also managed to spend some enjoyable time with other people and with God. Remember, you'll have more to give if you take care of yourself too.

Guilt-Free Mothering

I was talking to a woman at a Saturday morning church event when I noticed how often she mentioned that she really should get a part-time job. Her three children are in high school and college now, she volunteers as a teacher for English as a Second Language at her church, teaches a women's Bible study, and coordinates two short-term missions trips each year for her church. She occasionally travels with her husband on business trips and helps entertain clients.

Until the last year, Beth had her own painting and wallpapering business with a friend. Her friend moved away, and it seemed a good time for Beth to move on to other activities since the family didn't really need her extra income anymore.

But as we talked, she said at least three times, "I really should get a part-time job, but I just don't seem to have time." I asked what her husband thought, and she said he didn't think she had time for a job either. By the third time she mentioned the part-time job, I realized she felt guilty. I asked if her family didn't need for her to have a part-time job and she was doing other worthwhile activities that utilized her gifts and strengths, why did she feel that she needed to work?

So often we mothers feel as though we need to do more, we need to earn money, we need to be employed, and I'm sad that we don't think the myriad activities of motherhood are sufficient validation of our existence. Working is fine, often necessary, and rewarding in its own way, but let's not "guilt" ourselves into always thinking we're not doing quite enough. (My children have convinced me that "guilt" can be either a noun or a verb.)

I've been a stay-at-home mom and an employed mom, and both situations involve plenty of responsibility to keep a woman busy. So, can we ease up on our expectations for ourselves and let ourselves feel complete in whatever we're doing? I for one am determined to accept myself as I am today, doing what I can, loving my family, being productive, but not driving myself by constantly thinking I should do more.

How about you? Are you content knowing you're a valuable contributor to your family, to your workplace if you work, to your church or volunteer organization? Or do you berate yourself with silent self-talk that goes something like this, "I really should _____ (you fill in the blank)." Maybe it's time to reevaluate your activities and responsibilities and make a firm decision to give up guilt. Life's a lot better without it.

> What does the LORD require of you but to do justice, to love kindness, and to walk humbly with your God?
> —MICAH 6:8

One Hilarious Workout

Why does everything seem so serious these days? I'm serious about my work. I'm serious about mothering. I'm serious about exercise—well, sort of. And I even take seriously the joy of gardening. I think it's time to lighten up a bit. After all, I don't really need to review and recite my to-do list while I'm weeding.

Laughter reduces stress, promotes physical healing, is essential for mental health, and can add years to one's life. If a person laughs 100 times in a day, the effects equal ten minutes of strenuous rowing. And I'd much rather laugh than row strenuously.

When our eyes water during laughter, the tears contain stress hormones that are being released. When our faces flush with a hearty laugh, our cardiovascular systems get a workout, circulation improves, and our diaphragms massage our internal organs. Laughter also produces endorphins, natural painkillers that protect the immune system.

But life's problems and burdens often make it hard to find things funny. Norman Cousins, a chronic pain sufferer and author of *Anatomy of an Illness*, found that if he watched two hours of funny videos like *Candid Camera,* he could get two hours of pain-free sleep. If he watched the videos with another person, he could sleep pain-free even longer.

Humor is a perspective on life. It doesn't mean trivializing life's traumas, but rather turning negatives into positives. It's not making fun or mocking, but rather laughing *with* one another.

We can find humor by spending time with others who like to laugh and by learning to laugh at ourselves and stop being self-critical. We can read the comics, browse through humorous greeting cards, or purchase a joke book.

I know you're expecting me to make you laugh here pretty soon. Though I'm not much of a joke-teller, here goes (I have adapted this from www.geocities.com/Heartland/Farm):

The phone rang, and I was relieved to hear that kindly, maternal voice on the other end. "How are you, my girl?" it said. "How is your day going?"

I tearfully replied, "Oh, Mother, I've had such a bad day. The baby won't eat and the washing machine broke down. I haven't had time to go shopping, and, besides, I've just sprained my ankle and have to hobble around. Plus, the house is a mess, and I'm supposed to have two couples over for dinner tonight."

Mother was shocked and completely sympathetic. "Just sit down, dear, relax, and close your eyes. I'll be over in half an hour. I'll do your shopping, clean the house, and fix dinner for you. I'll feed the baby and call a repairman I know about your washing machine. I'll take care of everything for you, poor thing. I'll even call Ed and ask him to bring home some flowers for the table."

"Ed?" I asked. "Who's Ed?"

"Why, Ed, your husband." There was a moment of silence. "Is this 223-1374?"

"No, it's 322-1374."

"Oh, I'm sorry. I must have the wrong number."

Devastated, I asked, "Does this mean you're not coming over?"

Yes, on an especially stressful day, relief from *anyone*'s mother would be welcome. But maybe if I can laugh more and hurry less, even the stressful days will be better.

> A joyful heart is good medicine, but a
> broken spirit dries up the bones.
> —PROVERBS 17:22

Creative or Crazy?

Mothers of young children can get together with another mom or two so that the kids can play together and the moms can be together as well. When my children were in grade school, I used to take them with two other moms, Monique and Sherri, and their children up to Michigan to pick blueberries for one weekend each summer. We'd load all nine kids into two vans, drive four hours, and stay in one hotel room to save money. We'd pick pounds and pounds of plump, delicious blueberries for eating, cooking, and freezing at a fraction of what we would have paid in the grocery store.

Sure it was crowded, the kids sometimes fussed at and argued with each other, and we didn't get very much sleep with 12 people in the room, but we had so much fun talking and laughing together. And the memories of our blueberry picking trips that we made for our children are still talked about today.

Boys and Snakes

These same 12 people occasionally went out to Galena, Illinois, when we had a vacation home there, and the six boys went out hiking and exploring in the woods while the three girls put on nail polish in my daughter's room. The boys often found wild turkey feathers or a deer's skull in the woods, and they brought them back like prized trophies.

We had heard that rattlesnakes inhabited the area before people began to build cabins there, so we kept the weeds around the house cut down and warned the children about snakes. But my older son Andrew was—and is—fearless when it comes to wild animals. He loves nature and loves to collect shells and other specimens for what he used to say was going to be his very own museum.

The three moms were drinking coffee in the cabin one afternoon when we heard the boys stomping excitedly on the front porch and yelling for us to come see what they had found. We opened the front door and saw two of the boys with scratched and bleeding arms. One of them was my Andrew, who held a large snake triumphantly over his head. Three gasps warned the kids that we moms were not amused. We made him drop the snake and then tried to figure out whether it was a rattler. Andrew said it most definitely was not. But we had two bleeding boys, and we knew we needed to take them to the doctor. We also knew the doctor would ask what kind of snake it was.

The three of us looked at each other, shrugged, and Monique went into the kitchen, got a butcher knife, and proceeded to kill the snake so we could take it with us to the hospital. To our horror, the poor thing turned out to be pregnant, and Monique had performed an accidental Caesarean section on her. But we had our snake to show to the emergency room doctor, who agreed with my son that it was definitely not a rattler but rather a common garden snake.

The lesson to be learned from this story is to always take a snake guidebook with you when you go near woods with boys. And remember that some of your best memories with both your friends and family will come from surprise "disasters" as in this story.

Mission Impossible

The next story has to do with friendship only in an oblique way, but it has been told and retold at women's gatherings I've been a part of and has brought more friends into my circle.

My son Andrew, the future museum curator, was fascinated by the Field Museum of Natural History in Chicago. We took him there at least once a month when he was in elementary school, and he loved the huge dinosaur skeletons and the stuffed wild animals. He really wanted some like them for his own collection, and his father and I explained that getting one was pretty unlikely. He asked how they get the animals to look so real, and we gave a brief explanation of taxidermy. Well, that was what Andrew decided to do as soon as he was big enough; he was going to learn how to perform taxidermy so he could have a life-size animal of his very own. We already had a dog, so it wasn't as if the child was animal-deprived.

Andrew always felt badly when we saw a road-killed raccoon, and he asked several times if we couldn't have one of them preserved for his collection. I always shuddered and said no until the day we spotted a perfect raccoon, which looked as though he had just fainted on the side of the road. No blood or mess at all. Andrew got very excited, asking if we couldn't get it taxidermied, and in a moment of madness, I said we'd try it.

I drove home, got a couple of white plastic garbage bags and a plastic wastebasket, returned to the place where this perfect specimen lay on the side of the road, and instructed the children to stay safely in the car while I tried to scoop him up, which I was able to do without touching anything.

Andrew was beside himself, and it was worth it just to see the child so thrilled. We put the double-bagged raccoon in our Deepfreeze in the garage and started calling taxidermists in the yellow pages. Unfortunately, with quotes upwards of $500, we finally had to throw the poor fellow away, amidst tears and disappointment for my boy. We do look back on the memory with fondness, however, and I became somewhat famous at our school because of it, making several friends of women who sought me out to find out if the tale was actually true.

Sappy and Sweet

I have a group of friends called "Happy Hearts Too." Very corny, I know. All eight of us served together at our kids' elementary school on the Women's Auxiliary Board, and at the end of our term together, the speaker at our spring salad supper told us that her mother, now in her seventies, had met with several of her friends for 40 years. The group called themselves "Happy Hearts."

The eight of us decided that night that we would continue meeting, even though our time of service was now over, and that we would continue in the sappy tradition of "Happy Hearts," calling ourselves "Happy Hearts Too." We have continued to meet every month or two on a Saturday morning at 7:30 A.M. at a local restaurant. It's rare when all eight of us can make it, with kids' and husbands' schedules to work around, but whoever can come does, and we always have a good time.

Usually we go around the circle, giving updates on our families and a prayer request or two. We all usually get oatmeal, being a health-conscious group, although a couple of us split the feta cheese-spinach omelette. Whoever has to leave early does that, and the rest stay until about 9:30.

By getting Happy Hearts on our calendars, rather than letting it be crowded out, we continue this tradition that is important to all of us.

Do you have a group of friends who really belong on your calendar for regular get-togethers? I bet they'll love the idea when you suggest it to them.

> Pleasant words are a honeycomb, sweet to
> the soul and healing to the bones.
> —PROVERBS 16:24

Service with a Smile

One of the most fun ways to spend time with friends is by serving together. When we were in the Women's Auxiliary for our children's school, we built close relationships by doing for others. Our group prayed regularly for families with illnesses or job losses, and we lined up volunteer moms to take meals to these families, sometimes for extended periods of time to help them through a crisis. We organized break times for the teachers where a mom would relieve a teacher for part of the class lunch period so she could have some quiet time by herself. We provided hot lunches once a month for the kids (our school didn't have a cafeteria), and we brought in pizzas for another special monthly lunch.

Fundraising was part of our job, and we had craft sales and wrapping paper sales, and the money allowed the school to do extra things that would otherwise have been impossible. One year we contributed computer equipment; another year we gave each teacher a dollar amount to use for items needed for the classroom. But I think the rest of the women would agree with me that the best times were doing small, practical acts to help a family or an individual and seeing the smile or the look of relief we would get from the recipient.

One of the best ways to build relationships and spend time with friends is to serve together, whether it's at church, at school, in your neighborhood, for a charitable organization, or simply as individuals identifying needs and filling them. And you'll be providing a good example for your children too as they see you quietly and generously serving others.

> **Remember your friends:** Take your camera along next time you get together with one or more friends. Have the film developed and make as many prints as there are friends in the photo. Frame the pictures inexpensively and present one to each of your friends at the next event—birthday or Christmas—or for no occasion at all.

Special Delivery

I've never used a grocery delivery service, but I bet such a service would really be nice if you have a newborn or a sick child or you're sick yourself.

I have been the recipient of helpful neighbors or friends who, when I had an infant and only one car, which my husband took to work, would ask me if I could use anything from the store because they were going and could pick up a few things for me. What a treat!

I've tried to remember to do that occasionally for new moms in my neighborhood. Not only can I make a difference in the exhaustion level of a woman who may be up every couple of hours feeding her infant, but I often make a new friend at the same time.

Friends for Life

My mother kept in touch with her high school friends for more than 50 years. Three years ago Mother and I flew from Illinois to her hometown, Mobile, Alabama, for a get-together with her girlfriends. When Mother's friends told the skinny-dipping story on her, I was shocked...well, not really. I always knew she had a secret, spirited side despite her ladylike, steel magnolia façade.

If you think "Happy Hearts Too" is bad, Mother's six girl-friends had been calling themselves "Groaning Grannies" until they recently updated the name to a more becoming "Aging Angels."

Mother's friend Frances told a story from their high school days in 1944. "We were skinny-dipping in the Gulf (of Mexico) one afternoon when a busload of sailors drove up. All the girls got out of the water and ran to the beach house—all but your mother. She kept right on swimming, undisturbed, thinking the sailors would soon drive on up the beach.

"But the boys got out of the bus and started walking toward the water where she was swimming. She scrambled out of the water and crawled in the sand on her stomach toward the house, calling for somebody to throw her a cover.

"By this time the rest of us were wrapped up in Indian blankets, and one of us tossed one to your mother. She wrapped up in it and calmly walked the rest of the way to the house. When she got to where we were all standing and watching her, she raised her right hand and said, 'How' and walked into the house without another word."

That was Mother's humor, understated and dry. The reunited friends were just teenage girls in older bodies. They joked that they had been born in '72, not '27. They talked and laughed about things high school girls would talk and laugh about, at least in their day.

I sure hope I'm still getting together with my pals 50-plus years after high school. I skipped most of my high school reunions, but I began going again in the last few years. My class has a website, and many of us have begun to correspond again. Renewing old friendships has brought an added dimension of fun and reconnection to my life.

> There are three things that will endure—faith, hope, and love—and the greatest of these is love.
> —1 Corinthians 13:13 NLT

Better to Give

I have to tell you about my friend Chana (pronounced Hana) from Israel. Chana's husband, Chuck, told a very funny joke (even if I don't agree with its theology) at a fundraising dinner for her charitable organization, Saret, which she started in order to help poor people who can't pay rent or utilities because of job loss or illness.

Chuck said, "A group of Hadassah ladies [a Jewish women's group named for Esther in the Bible] arrived at the pearly gates but were turned down for admittance by Saint Peter. They were sent to the hot department down below, but several days later Peter found some new information and called down to Satan to send them on back up. Satan said, 'No way am I sending them back up. They've been here just three days, and they've already raised $100,000 for air conditioning.'"

Chana, too, is tireless on behalf of others. She is a court watcher, observing the judicial system and supporting people going through the system for divorce or child custody matters; she writes dozens of letters to the editor about issues and abuses she believes need changing; she produces cable TV programs about health and political issues. She raises money for her Saret clients who have major life problems and can't make ends meet. She helps people find alternative remedies for health problems at no charge, and she makes a point of learning about candidates in elections and then lobbying her friends and acquaintances to vote for her choices. All this while teaching 34 piano students and being a wife and the mother of three nearly grown children.

Observing Chana, I realize that while I sometimes feel busy and stressed, it's important and valuable to make time in a busy schedule to help those who need it. And when my problems seem overwhelming, if I sit down and list what I'm thankful for, my perspective changes from "poor me" to "grateful me."

Break for Lunch

According to Dr. Michael F. Roizen, author of *RealAge: Are You as Young as You Can Be?*[1], having supportive friendships and family relationships can take three and a half years off a person's age. Couple that with taking care of my emotional health, which reduces real age by a whopping 16 years, and I'm really a very young woman.

Because exercise and friendship go together well, several women in my office gather to walk at lunchtime. We put on our running shoes and head for our warehouse in the winter or outside in the warmer weather for a brisk half-hour walk. It's a great way to squeeze some movement into your day, whether you work out later or not.

Besides having fun talking with each other, we stretch our muscles and give our brains a nice oxygen boost so we're refreshed and alert for the rest of our day.

Surprise Sighting

One of my favorite occurrences is seeing someone I love where and when I didn't expect to, like running into a friend at the coffee shop or seeing my brother walking home from work when I'm driving around town. It's hard to describe, but I get a feeling that's a moment of lightness, like a cool breeze that ripples by unexpectedly on a hot day. I think this is somewhat of a personal quirk because I don't see other people seeming as thrilled as I am when they run into ME.

When I was married, we went to stay at our summer home for a month. I knew no one in that town, and after a couple of weeks I was really missing the way I run into people I know all the time at home. One day I was in the grocery store in the little town near the cottage, and I saw a mother from my children's school who happened to be vacationing there. I'm sure she thought I was very weird because I was so happy to see her, I nearly knocked her over. But seeing people I know is something I really like.

While I can't plan to run into someone accidentally, I can spontaneously call a friend and ask if she has 20 minutes to have coffee or take a walk with me. Even a few minutes with someone I love can change the way I look at my day.

Letting Her Talk

"If Christians can't get it together, what hope is there?" my friend Claire asked. "My Christian neighbors are divorcing; Christian kids I know are getting into trouble; another Christian couple is separated because of physical abuse; a Christian woman is in her third unhappy marriage. Christian friends have hurt me with thoughtless words. Where is the victory in all that?"

Tears filled her big, blue eyes and threatened to overflow onto her pale cheeks. "I'm sad about all the Christian failure I see around me."

I mentally clicked on my internal "find" command and started scanning comforting words and verses about encouragement and trusting God.

But those brimming blue eyes checked my words. I don't have the answer, the reason for the bad things that happen. What I can say she already knows. She's memorized Romans 8:28 ("And we know that God causes all things to work together for good to those who love God, to those who are called according to His purpose") and Philippians 4:13 ("I can do all things through Him who strengthens me"). She knows that much evil results from sin.

I decided to just touch her arm and listen. I said, "I understand. I know. I feel the same way sometimes."

I wanted to go into my "count your blessings" lecture, but I held myself back.

How about my "trust God anyway" talk?

Nah—she delivers that one to her kids often.

I know, the "God's in control" speech. Not now.

I let her talk. I put away my speeches, turned off my mental computer, and listened. And I began to hear, really hear, her pain and frustration. I realized that when I'm mentally searching and sorting and planning how to fix it, I'm not really hearing, absorbing, or feeling what my friend is saying.

Finally, I simply said, "I don't have any answers, but God does." I tried to give her permission to hurt, to feel pain, to admit her questions and her grief.

That day I learned an important lesson. Letting someone talk without trying to provide answers is often the right thing to do. Friends have done this for me, and I now practice trying to just listen, be quiet, and offer my presence and my prayers to a hurting person.

❧   ❧   ❧

> **Remember your friend:** While you're gardening, dig up part of a perennial plant, wrap its roots in a damp paper towel enclosed in a plastic bag, and drop it off at a friend's house with a note saying it's from you and what kind of plant it is (if you know).

Saying Thanks

I never thought I would quit writing thank-you notes. My mother drilled it into us that it was what a well-mannered person always did, without fail, no matter what. Failure to write a thank-you note meant you were ungrateful for the time, effort, and money expended for you—either that or you were just plain rude.

When I had my own children, I laboriously urged them to write thank-you notes from the smallest ages, when they could barely write, and I'm glad I did it. I think it teaches the importance of expressing gratitude and taking the time to do it in a memorable way. I used to bribe them by giving them a small piece of candy upon the completion of each note that read something like, "Dear Aunt Sally: Thank you for the nice Lego set you gave me for my birthday. I really like it. Love, Steve."

This year my 16-year-old son, Andrew, wrote notes for his birthday gifts with no nagging from me. I didn't even mention it because lately I've been thinking that it's enough to thank people warmly in person or by phone when you receive a gift. But I was thrilled when he even handed me, his mother, a handwritten note!

I don't write as many thank-you notes as I used to, but I still love getting one just as much as I ever did. I have a red folder crammed with notes I've saved over the years. Rereading some of them can bring tears to my eyes.

How about taking a minute today to write a note to someone who has meant a lot to you? Thank him (or her) specifically for something he did in your life that made a difference, like the time he encouraged you when no one else thought you could become captain of the soccer team. Or the time she believed in you when you took that art class.

Come to think of it, I'm going to reevaluate my decision to ease up on writing thank-you notes. There's really nothing like the happy, appreciated feeling you get when you receive one.

Friendship Online

I love e-mail. I like it because in seconds I can correspond with a friend without pen and paper and stamps. I also like it because I can compose my thoughts and revise what I'm saying in a way I can't do when speaking to someone. And of course I like it because it's fast and cheap.

When my friend Carol moved to Texas, I feared losing touch with her, but we e-mail often and send each other family updates and prayer requests. My mother's friend Carol

Thoms keeps me supplied with good, clean jokes, and another friend sends me health tips regularly.

If you're not hooked up to the Internet, I'd suggest that you consider such a step. Just keep the computer in a part of the house where you are aware of what the children are doing on it. It's easy for them to accidentally stumble onto something you wouldn't want them to see.

Pampered Pals

Is there anything more luxurious than a massage? One time my friend Sherri gave me a gift certificate for a one-hour massage, and I enjoyed every knead of my tired, old muscles. At the end of the hour I was as limp as a dishrag—or microfiber cloth—as relaxed as I could remember ever feeling.

If you can't afford a gift like that (and I can't), offer to help paint or wallpaper a room or take care of your friend's kids while she has a couple of hours to herself. There are many ways to pamper your friends. When Kathleen walks in and I have dirty dishes (more often than I'd like to admit), she just washes them for me without even asking.

Just as important as giving is being able to graciously receive help or gifts or kindness from others. If it's hard to let someone do something for you, imagine yourself in the giver's place and decide to let her have the joy that comes from giving to you.

> **Remember your friend:** Next time you get together, take a half dozen homemade cookies wrapped in plastic wrap and tied with a ribbon. Attach a recipe card containing the cookie recipe to the ribbon.

Different Perspectives

I heard a good example of the difference between positive and negative thinking when I took a bouquet of flowers to my mother in the nursing home. Mother was sitting in the main activity room when I arrived. She smiled when she saw me with the flowers and said, "Thank you." I started to tell her they were from the yard when a woman sitting near Mother said, "What beautiful flowers." I smiled, thanked her, and said they were from my yard. A third woman nearby said, "But when you cut them, they don't last very long after that. They'll be dead soon."

What a difference in response to cut flowers! I believe it's important to steer my mind and attitude in the right direction and form some good thinking habits now while I'm young (sort of), so that when I'm older my thoughts will be pleasant and sweet instead of snarly and sour.

I think I'm much more likely to keep my friends later on if I am someone who is enjoyable to be around and not a big grouch.

More Month than Money

My mother had a friend in New Jersey named Jane. Jane's husband was an FBI agent, as was my stepfather, so the men knew each other as well. They had children similar in age; Jane with three girls, my mother with two girls and two boys.

Their friendship reminded me of Lucille Ball and Ethel Mertz in the *I Love Lucy* show. They were always laughing at the funny dinner combinations they had to feed their families when it grew close to payday—meals like scrambled eggs with salami and canned soup with applesauce.

They lived on cash and wouldn't have thought of charging groceries on a credit card, even if that option had even been available back then. But they got together with all seven kids and took us to the shore occasionally, picnic baskets and all. They got together as couples too, and even when Jane and her husband, Mick, were transferred to a different part of the country from my parents, they all stayed in touch and visited each other whenever they had the chance.

I guess I came by my high valuation of friendship and camaraderie honestly; I had a good example to follow. Now it's my turn to remember that my children, too, are learning about the value of friends as they watch me with mine.

Friends and Neighbors

The day I went into the hospital to have my third child, Steve, our Volkswagen Rabbit broke down. At the time we were a one-car family, and the repair shop told my husband it was hopeless. Our next-door neighbor at the time, Joe, brought over the keys to his car and simply gave them to my husband without comment. No instructions or warnings on how to use it or to be careful with it, just the keys, and "Congratulations on the birth of your new son. Keep the car as long as you need it."

That kind of neighborliness breeds friendship. In our neighborhood we shared extension ladders, snowblowers, and weed whackers so that we didn't all have to purchase the tools. And some of the best times I've had have been when a friend needed a ride to pick up her car being serviced or gave me a ride to mine.

If you watch out for opportunities to help or share what a neighbor may need, new or strengthened friendships will follow you no matter where you live.

Give and Get

As I've already said, one of the most important keys to real living is doing for others. When you help someone else, you get a certain feeling inside that is like no other—it's as though your heart is smiling, and it tightens a little bit with the joy you feel. Either that or you're having a heart attack, and you'd better rush to the hospital.

My two teenage sons, bless their hearts, used to go over to my sister's every Friday night to help her. Sally is a story in her own right. She survived schizophrenia, two divorces from the same mean man, cancer, and poverty. She lived in subsidized housing on her Social Security disability checks supplemented by her work as a grocery store cashier. She was one of the most generous people I've ever known, and my children recognize this. One year she gave my daughter a fabulous "Wedding Barbie," and she always managed to give big and wonderful gifts to all her nieces and nephews for Christmas and their birthdays. I don't know how she did it.

Anyway, Andrew and Steve went on Fridays to carry her soda cans from her car to her third-floor apartment and take out garbage for her. She had a broken hip and a bad back from spinal stenosis, and she was not supposed to lift or carry heavy objects. It was almost a miracle that she even let them do this for her because she was fiercely independent and never wanted to put anyone out to help her.

One Friday she mentioned that if she could save money on her insurance premiums, she was going to buy herself a new twin bed she had seen on sale to replace the fold-up cot she slept on.

So the next day my sons and I bought her a twin bed—mattress, box springs, and frame—and I charged it, which I really shouldn't have done on my budget. We took it over in my old minivan and knocked on her door. Of course she objected when she saw us carrying in a mattress, but we convinced her to let us do it. The boys set it up, and she cried the whole time they were there.

The three of us left her apartment considerably lighter emotionally. Giving is one of the most important keys to real living.

Car Praying

All the mothers whose children lived too far away to walk to my kids' elementary school drove them, either alone or in a carpool, because we didn't have buses. One year several of us met every Wednesday fifteen minutes before the kids got out of school. We'd pile into one car and pray for all the children of these mothers. Not only did we build our friendships, but we were also able to lift our concerns for our children up to God on a regular basis. We knew that where two or more are gathered...he answers.

Walking with a Friend

My favorite exercise is walking. Even in cold weather, it's invigorating to bundle up well and head out for a walk. It's one of my favorite times to talk to God too. Often I talk to him during my entire 45-minute walk, even though praying for 45 minutes when I'm in the house seems almost impossible.

On my walks I usually start out with, "It's me, Barbara, Lord," and then I talk to him about my children first. I imagine his big, strong, and capable hands, and then I place each one of the children into them, as if they're the tiny children in *Honey, I Shrunk the Kids*. I ask God to help them be healthy in all of these ways: physically, emotionally, mentally, spiritually, psychologically, relationally, socially, financially, and vocationally. I think that pretty well covers the areas of their lives in which I long for them to be healthy and successful. If anyone has additional areas to add, please let me know, because I sure want to cover it all with God for my kids.

Then I talk to him about each one of them individually, what they're doing, what their needs are, what I'm concerned about. And I ask him to help me be the mother he wants me to be, wise and kind, loving and firm and fun.

I then talk to God about my friends and their needs and problems. I turn to my work and talk to God about that, and then my finances. Sometimes that issue takes up several blocks of my walk. I try to thank him right along as I ask for things because I know I'd surely get tired of hearing my kids beg me for thing after thing without a little gratitude mixed in with it; but, of course, he's not me and he loves to hear our prayers, again and again, all the time. I really appreciate that about him.

I pray for our country and our leaders, my church and my neighbors, and by that time I'm usually back home. There's nothing quite as nice as a lovely, long walk with a Friend.

Batter Up

Think back to a time when one of your kids did something outstanding. Maybe it was a piano recital when she really shone, or a hockey game where he scored the winning goal, or the day your toddler spent as long as he could sit still making a beautiful picture just for you. Remember the feeling you had? The feeling of joy and pride and pleasure that he had done so well?

When my son Steve was 11, he played on a community baseball team, complete with team T-shirts, black baseball pants, baseball shoes with cleats, and matching caps. I always enjoyed taking my folding chair and sitting on the sidelines with the other parents, all of us hoping our kids would do well and have fun.

Steve was a very good player, but he had his share of strikeouts and fumbles too. He often got solid hits, but some were caught before he could get on base. One evening he approached the plate, grabbed his bat, wiggled into his stance, and held the bat high behind his head, looking at that pitcher and concentrating for all he was worth. I knew he really wanted to do well, and I, like parents everywhere, long for successes for my children, those events that build confidence and help them believe they can do something well.

The bases were loaded. The pitcher nodded to the catcher and fired a good pitch right past Steve. *Give him a hit, Lord; encourage my boy.* The next pitch also sailed right by him and into the catcher's mitt as Steve swung like Mark McGwire—he really did. He was always a good sport about losses, but I knew he could really use the encouragement of a win tonight.

He leaned into his stance and chewed his gum ferociously. *Help him, Lord.*

As the pitch whipped over the base, Steve swung and the bat struck the ball perfectly. He dropped the bat and headed for first base as fast as he could go. One runner came in. The outfielders scrambled to get on the ball, but it seemed to sail past them. The second runner crossed the plate. One of the outfielders turned around and chased after the ball that seemed to be propelled by a little invisible motor, and the third runner crossed home plate.

We were all on our feet, screaming, cheering, and clapping for my boy. Of course, tears came to my eyes because

I knew how much this would mean to him. When Steve was just leaving third, the outfielder whipped the ball toward home, and Steve and that ball ran neck and neck to see who could get there first. He slid over the base like a pro, and the stands and his team went wild. I wish you could have seen how tall he stood when the game was over and it was time to go home.

I was so proud of my boy, proud and pleased that he had a personal victory that evening. On the way home, I thought of God cheering me on when I'm trying to accomplish something, when he knows I need a win. And as I felt my heart expand with pleasure and pride for my son, I thought I had a tiny taste of what he must feel like when I get a grand-slam home run in some area of my endeavors, even if it's rare and unexpected, even if he gave me the bat and the shoes and the nutrition and the practice sessions that made it happen. His parent's heart still swells like mine did that night, because my boy experienced a triumph he would never forget.

Thank you, God, for cheering us on.

Little Flowers

It was the dead of winter when I went out onto my sun-porch to water plants I bring in from outside in the fall. The plants look wilted and half dead during the winter, but if I water them anyway, when I take them back out in the spring, they recover and look great again. So I went to water the dilapidated plants on the porch, and I saw that one lifeless, pitiful vine had produced three lovely purple flowers, all stretching their little necks up toward the sun.

Maybe you're thinking I put too much meaning into a little thing like that, but I felt as though God had put those three little flowers there to encourage me about my three children. I trust that my children are stretching their little necks—well, their necks are not so little anymore—toward the Son, Jesus Christ.

God is watching over them and looking out for them. He comforts me often with the words from Jeremiah 24:6-7: "My eyes will watch over them for their good, and I will bring them back to this land. I will build them up and not tear them down; I will plant them and not uproot them. I will give them a heart to know me, that I am the LORD. They will be my people, and I will be their God, for they will return to me with all their heart" (NIV).

Time to Be Still

One summer I worked especially hard in my yard. Often I eagerly and enthusiastically plant my annuals around Mother's Day and then lose much of my interest in gardening except to expect the flowers to bloom untended and unweeded.

But a few years ago I maintained my energy and zeal through and beyond the Fourth of July. Every day I pulled a few weeds, watered, and planted perennials I bought on sale or received as a cutting from a friend. I studied books on perennial gardening, analyzed what would grow well in my yard, fertilized, and ran out each morning to see what had bloomed since yesterday.

While I did have some limited success, the rabbits in my neighborhood outwitted me. Many mornings I would come out to find petunias and phlox gnawed off as if surgically excised. I sprinkled blood meal and organic pest deterrents, installed little cages around the plants, and tied a metal pie pan on a string to a tomato cage so it would blow around and act like a scarecrow. But the rabbits prevailed. The only flowers that did well were those rabbits didn't care for.

One day, after a discouraging round with the little brown beasts, I noticed a small spot in the yard which is hidden and out of the way. I almost never see it because it's not prominent or noticeable, and I don't walk to that corner unless I'm chasing a ball. As I looked into the little dark place, something white caught my eye. I went closer, pulled back some weeds and branches that had overgrown the area, and found a lush, wild green vine covered with white trumpetlike flowers that reminded me of pale morning glories. I had never planted them or noticed them there before. I stopped to admire and study their profusion. *Why can't the ones I work on do this well?* I wondered.

I realized that God had provided much more than all my work could accomplish, and without any effort on my part. Psalm 46:10 came to me: "Cease striving, and know that I am God," and I smiled. Work and effort are good and necessary, but there is a time to be still and know that he is God.

❀ ❀ ❀

A Simple Job

I took in the bedroom shades to be fixed. The store clerk said, "No, they must be replaced. There is no way to repair them."

I purchased new shades, the man cut them to match my old shades, and I went home. Because I had covered the old shades with fabric to match my bedspread, I had to remove the fabric and sew it onto the new ones before I could hang them. I sat down in a kitchen chair to sew the fabric on by hand.

It took me ten minutes to thread the needle the first time. Then the thread knotted up on my second stitch. I began sewing again and realized I had sewed the fabric on the wrong way; I had to tear it out and start over. This time I sewed it crooked; I started over again.

Then I noticed that the horizontal wood slat in the bottom of the shade that allows me to pull it up and down was too long. It had not been properly trimmed off at the store and stuck out on both sides of the shade. I went out to the garage, found a branch-trimming tool, and clipped the wood off so that it would fit the opening without protruding.

I finally had the fabric on and the shade ready to hang. I started up the stairs to the bedroom. On the way, the shade, which was slightly wider than the stair hallway, got stuck and, as I tried to free it, I broke the wooden slat I had just lopped off with the trimmer.

Exasperated, I decided to hang the shade anyway and fix the wood another time. At least I'd be able to sleep tonight with my windows covered. I hung the shade and saw that it was cut too narrow. The hardware didn't reach far enough to go into the wall bracket. So I bent in the metal holders to make them accommodate the narrow shade.

At last, I had the shade reinstalled. But it wouldn't move up and down. After more work and improvisation, I fixed it. This simple job had taken hours to accomplish.

This annoying experience reminded me how glad I am that God doesn't get frustrated with me and toss me away in despair or just leave me in my broken state, not quite working right. Instead, he who began a good work in me will be faithful to complete it (see Philippians 1:6).

Slowing Down

It was dark and I was writing by candlelight, which I knew was an unhealthy thing to do. John Milton went blind, and the cause is thought to have been reading for countless hours by candlelight. But Abe Lincoln did it, and it didn't seem to harm him. Anyway, this once wouldn't hurt me, I thought.

Our electricity had been out for about four hours. I was writing an article when the lights browned and then blacked out. It was broad daylight, so there was still plenty to do without electricity. The children weren't home. First, I went out and divided hostas in my yard—cheap landscaping. I planted them where all that seems to grow is weeds and suckers. The hostas are so hearty that my mother once dug some up to divide and left them unplanted in an old bushel basket all winter. Amazingly, they came back to life the next spring, right there in the old basket, bare roots and all.

Then I washed up and loaded the dishwasher and cleaned the kitchen. The water worked fine. A family in the next town had an electric well instead of city water. Last fall their power was out for four days, during which they couldn't use the toilets, take a shower, or wash dishes. They finally rented a generator just to enjoy indoor plumbing again. I was glad to have water on this day of no electricity.

Until it grew dark I sat on the porch proofreading my article. I could see and hear my neighbors out on their back decks, all of us driven outside by the dark stillness in our homes. The next-door neighbors were out with both their children, and I wondered if they were appreciating the blackout because it made the four of them sit outside talking together with no music, TV, or indoor chores or pastimes demanding attention.

As night fell I strained to keep reading and rewriting on the porch, but it eventually became impossible.

I came in and made a list of all the things I take for granted yet was unable to do because of the power outage.

- ❀ I can't drive anywhere because my overhead garage door opener is electric. I know there's a manual switch, but I don't know how to use it, and I don't want to try to find the operating instructions by flashlight or break the opener trying.

- ❀ I can't write on my computer. I can't wash or dry laundry or cook. I can't tell time except by my watch, which conveniently lights up at the press of a little button.

- ❀ I can't read unless I want to wind up like Milton.

❀ I can't vacuum, I realize with relief. I hope the food in the refrigerator and freezer doesn't spoil.

❀ I can't turn on the air-conditioning or a fan, and it's about 90 degrees.

❀ I can't listen to music or watch TV. The sump pump is on battery backup, so the only sound in the house is the high-pitched alarm telling me the backup is doing its job.

I laughed because we think we're so independent and self-sufficient, so technologically advanced. But God can drastically change our daily doings, shut them all down quickly, with just one little old storm. I was reminded of Proverbs 16:9, "The mind of man plans his way, but the LORD directs his steps." I was thankful that my real Power Source never fails, and I appreciated the gentle lesson of the dark.

You won't believe me, but as I wrote the word "dark," in longhand, the lights came back on. Honest.

God sometimes provides a needed break for us in ways we don't expect.

Shade

It feels as though it is a lot more than ten degrees cooler when you step under a tall oak whose broccoli branches stretch up toward the sun after you've been working in the garden or playing with your kids or watching a baseball game in the sun. Suddenly you sense relief from the heat and you're refreshed. You breathe in the cooler air and savor the breeze rustling the leaves.

Shade is delicious protection from scorching heat. Like a cool drink when you're thirsty, like a run through the sprinkler on a hot day, like an encouraging word from a friend, so is the cool relief of shade.

I used to complain that I was limited in my flower gardening because I had so much shade at our big house. I couldn't have roses or hollyhocks or daisies. My tomato plants were leggy vines with few tomatoes. Grass was harder to grow in shade. The man at the nursery told me that if his hardiest grass seed didn't take in my shade, I might as well blacktop the yard and give up on grass. Some of the rooms in my house were dark from the shade.

But the house stayed cool. We rarely needed the air-conditioning. Exterior paint lasts longer, as does the roof, if your yard is shady. I grew lush hosta, astilbe, ferns, pansies, impatiens, and begonias.

And sitting in the cool yard with loved ones or alone, looking up through a canopy of towering oaks to the sky beyond, was wonderful. The slightest breeze created the harmony of dancing leaves. It was peaceful and serene under the oaks' protection.

Yes, shade was a gift. Eventually I had to sell that house and purchase a smaller one. This house has a sun-filled yard full of rosebushes and all sorts of sun-loving plants like irises and black-eyed Susans.

I went from lovely shade to beautiful sun. There are benefits and drawbacks to both. The key, I learned, was to enjoy whichever one I was experiencing at the moment, rather than wishing for a sunnier or shadier yard.

Take a minute to thank God for both shade and sun and his provision of both.

> Let me, if I may, be ever welcomed to my room
> in winter by a glowing hearth, in summer by a
> vase of flowers; if I may not, let me then think
> how nice they would be, and bury myself in
> my work. I do not think that the road to
> contentment lies in despising what we have
> not got. Let us acknowledge all good, all delight
> that the world holds, and be content without it.
> —GEORGE MACDONALD in
> *Annals of a Quiet Neighborhood*

A Breakfast Surprise

In our community, the "biggest oak in town" is in Denise's back yard. A city official who came to measure it made this proclamation. She had her trees inspected for disease, damage, or carpenter ants annually because a number of trees in her neighborhood had these problems. The tree service always said her trees were healthy.

But at 7:00 one windy morning, her house shook as though a giant had stepped on it. She ran to her daughter's bedroom to see if she was safe. After checking on her, Denise looked out the upstairs back window to see what had happened.

The biggest oak in town had split in two, and half of it had fallen on her house. She ran downstairs to find debris all over the sunroom. Cracks zigzagged across the walls like spider veins. The windows angled crazily. A tree branch protruded right through the wall. She stepped outside to find her garden smashed and her deck damaged. The part of the fallen tree that hit her house was too big to wrap her arms around. Had it been another tree in the yard, it could have crushed 16-year-old Lindsay's bedroom with her in it.

Problems can come at us out of the blue. A relationship or even our own bodies that we believe are healthy can suddenly collapse like that giant oak did. While she suffered considerable damage to her house, yard, and wallet that day, Denise was overwhelmed with gratitude that the biggest oak in town had missed the two occupied bedrooms in her house, sparing her daughter's life and her own.

One of my favorite verses—and this one is sustaining me right now—is Psalm 112:7. I put myself right into the verse, "[I] will not fear evil tidings; [my] heart is steadfast, trusting in the LORD."

He Brings Me Flowers

I'd like to end this chapter with one of my favorite stories about my Very Best Friend. During my marriage, the year after we moved into my dream house, I planted a rose bush. The bush disappeared in our shady yard. Several years later when my marriage was falling apart and I felt too overwhelmed to do any yard work, my flower beds became jungles of weeds.

But one day I noticed something red in the weedy bed in the front yard, and I walked over to see what it was. I discovered a lone red rose amidst the debris, a faithful remnant of the bush I had planted so long ago.

I felt as though God was reminding me he was still there, in the middle of the weeds and thorns of my life, and that he would continue to surprise me with joys like this unexpected rose in the difficult days ahead. The little bush bloomed again and again during my remaining years in the house, and when I put the house on the market, one of the hardest things to leave was my rosebush. I knew that roses don't transplant well, and while the house was for sale, I frequently walked around the yard, winding up at the bush, crying and grieving my losses.

I sold the house to a lovely couple, but then I became worried. I prayed, "Where will I go, Lord? I've got three children and no place to go!" I had looked at houses I could afford, and many were dismal. As I got up off my knees, the phone rang, and it was a Realtor friend who said he had a few houses to show me that afternoon. I dreaded looking at more depressing places.

But when we stepped into the house I now own, I said immediately, "I want it." I didn't even go out to the yard or garage in my excitement over the meticulously maintained, charming home. The house had been on the market only three days, and we wrote a contract immediately.

Two weeks later, I met the couple who owned the house, and Mary, the wife, told me that she'd be trimming up the 13 rosebushes in the yard before she moved out. My eyes teared up as I realized that God had replaced my one rosebush with many more.

Yes, we can count on him—our Ultimate Friend—for joyful surprises even in the tough times.

❧   ❧   ❧

Are We There Yet?

Streamlining the Family Schedule

%% %% %%

The alarm went off at 6:15 A.M. I pushed the snooze button and turned over for that luscious "five more minutes." When the clock sounded its unwelcome news again, I dutifully got up, and the day's activities began marching through my mind. *Breakfast—let's have oatmeal and raisins. I think I have enough turkey left to use in their lunches. Yikes, Steve has to be there early this morning to take the test he missed when he was sick last week! I'd better hurry.*

My agenda continued as I got in the shower. *It's my turn to drive for Andrew's field trip this afternoon. What would I do if I didn't have a flexible job so I can leave early when I need to? Oh, and the library books are late; I need to drop them off and also pick up Ed's dry cleaning. He needs his gray suit for that meeting tonight, and he left so early this morning he couldn't get it himself. Then I'll pick up Carolyn from tennis practice and stop for milk.*

I stepped out of the shower, quickly dressed, put on the minimal makeup I wear, and wrapped six hot rollers in the ends of my hair. I called my two older children to wake up on my way down to the kitchen, knowing I'd have to make several more attempts before everyone actually got up. They had told me they were too big now for a wake-up kiss from their mom—except for Steve, who was eight. I entered his room and kissed him, saying, "Time to wake up, my boy," and wondered how long he'd keep letting me do that.

Downstairs I started the coffee, put a pot of oatmeal on to cook, and got out the lunch ingredients. *I really need to have them start fixing their own lunches.* I called upstairs several more times, and finally all three sat groggily at the table.

Breakfast done, I went into the laundry room to find two matching socks for Andrew, and as I rooted through clean clothes piled on top of the dryer, I heard a screech from the kitchen. "Mom, Sandy threw up. You'd better hurry. She looks like she's going to do it again!"

I dashed into the kitchen to find a very sick pewter-colored dog surrounded by three upset kids. By the time I cleaned that up and comforted the dog and the children, it was time for Carolyn and Andrew to get to the school bus. "Did you get your lunches?" I asked. I told Steve to head for the car, and I remembered the meeting I had scheduled for this morning at work. *Where is that report I worked on last night? It's due today and that was my only copy.* I frantically dug through papers on my kitchen desk, found the report, said goodbye to the two older children, and scrambled for the car, hoping Steve wouldn't be late for his makeup test.

"Mom, you've still got those *things* in your hair," he said. I snatched out my curlers, promising myself I'd brush my hair before I got to the office with the brush I kept in the car.

I backed out of the garage, mentally checking things off. *I turned off the stove and coffeepot; I'll go to the dry cleaners at lunchtime; don't forget the field trip.* The car was at the end of the driveway when Steve said, "Mom, I forgot my red folder, and I need it today." Back into the house we went, my frustration level rising quickly.

When I got to work, I grabbed my report from the floor of the car and rushed into the building. "Good morning, Barb," the receptionist greeted me. "It looks like you have a new hairstyle. I like it."

There's nothing like unbrushed hair to start your day off right. Have you ever had a morning like mine? If you're a mother, I'm sure you have. This chapter will give you a few ways to streamline your schedule, mostly methods I have come up with out of sheer desperation. I hope they help.

Helping Your Kids Get Themselves Up on Time

You're probably thinking that the first way I'm going to suggest to streamline your schedule is to give up curling your hair. While I do sometimes opt for the easier ponytail, the idea for today will help you get to work with your hair curled *and* brushed.

I took all three children to the store and let them each pick out an alarm clock. Steve's had a big friendly face and a loud clanging sound. Andrew's was small and black and cool, producing a sophisticated beep, and Carolyn's was a multicolored clock that made musical tones I didn't think would wake me up at all.

They felt pretty grown-up having their own alarm clocks, but I had to supplement this newfound responsibility with a system of bonus points for getting up on time. For every ten minutes they were late in the morning, they went to bed ten minutes earlier than usual that night. While this system didn't work perfectly and had to be restructured as they grew older, it gradually moved the job of getting the children up in the morning off of my To-Do list and onto theirs.

Things kids can do the night before a school day:

Lay out their clothes, avoiding the frantic search for matching socks in the morning. Designate one spot where they should put their clothes for tomorrow, including underwear and socks, before 7 P.M. the night before.

Pack up backpacks with all necessary papers, permission slips, books, pencils, and other equipment.

Make a sandwich, wash a piece of fruit, wrap a few cookies in plastic wrap or a plastic bag, put it all in a brown lunch bag with an individual size bag of chips. Put the entire bag into the refrigerator, ready for fast grabbing the next morning.

Housework: A Family Affair

Some mothers have more success at getting help with the housework from the kids than others do. When my friend Nancy from high school said her kids clear the dinner table, load the dishwasher, and later take turns putting the clean dishes away (when her kids were all in elementary school), I was impressed. My children mastered the act of carrying their dishes over to the countertop after meals at young ages, but often their idea of helping turned into having some rip-roaring fun at mom's expense. One of their favorites was putting dirty clothes down the clothes chute, which emptied into the laundry room. Not only would they sometimes put clean, folded clothes that they were supposed to put into drawers down the chute, but occasionally when I was in the laundry room, a large truck would come hurtling down the chute, making a loud crash behind me. I could hear the giggles coming from upstairs.

Another friend, Catherine, experienced some "help" she hasn't completely gotten over to this day. Her 11-year-old son and his friend wanted to help her get ready for a party, and they volunteered to vacuum the furniture in the family room. David and Matt set the canister on end and quickly realized the hilarity of putting the end of the vacuum cleaner hose on their stomachs, creating suction and many laughs. They did this repeatedly until both boys had red circles across their abdomens. They didn't realize, however, that as they blocked the flow of air into the vacuum cleaner, they forced lots of dirt out the other end of the canister and deep into the nice off-white Berber carpeting.

Catherine says that now, 13 years later, the stain is nearly gone, but you can still see it if the light in the family room is right.

So who says helping mom with her chores isn't fun?

❦   ❦   ❦

> **They *Try* to Help:**
>
> One Saturday evening I stopped at a gas station, asked my ten-year-old son to go in and get me a Sunday *Tribune*, and gave him money. In a few minutes he came out empty-handed, although I could see stacks of the thick papers in the store. He got into the car and said, "Sorry, Mom, they didn't have any."
>
> "Are you sure?" I asked.
>
> "I'm sure," he replied. "They didn't have any Sunday *Tribunes*. All they had were *Chicago Tribunes*."

Gainful Employment

One way to help children avoid boredom in the summer and learn the value of money is to help them work. I realize that the first time you make this suggestion, you may get a negative response, but keep at it. They can be won over to the idea.

My children often had lemonade stands, as little kids like to do, or they would make little clay objects and sell them. They had a great time doing this and felt very proud of their accomplishments. I had them pay a small amount for the ingredients they used so they would understand that products you sell must be purchased or made before you sell them and make a profit.

But when my sons reached ages ten and twelve, they wanted to start a lawn mowing business. We made up flyers and put them in mailboxes around the neighborhood, and they had several interested customers. Babysitting and petsitting are more good ways for young children to occupy their time profitably, earn a little money, and learn about providing a service for someone else.

Making Memorizing Easier

Finding time-saving homework techniques can add precious minutes to your family's schedule. A great way to help your kids memorize Bible verses or schoolwork is to put the verse to music. Make up a tune and sing the verse over and over until your child has it. Or she can make up the tune and sing it over and over until you beg her to stop. That way you both will learn the verse.

Another technique is to put the memory verse on a 3 x 5 card, put the card in a plastic zipper sandwich bag, and seal it. Then tape the bag onto the wall of the bathtub or shower and those long baths/showers will produce a learned verse. Taping them on the bathroom mirror works too. And some moms tape a verse on their steering wheel for their own memory work while they're driving. Just be sure to keep your eyes on the road and memorize at traffic lights only.

Sock Hungry

My daughter started doing her own laundry when she was about 11 and didn't like the way I would occasionally shrink things up by accident. Her help, of course, was fine with me. But she, too, learned what it's like to have the washer or dryer eat your socks and underwear so that you can never find them again.

One way to keep socks together through the wash is to pin them with safety pins or clip them together with clothes-pins. But the clothespins sometimes come off, and the safety pin attachment is time-consuming.

The answer is one of those permanent laundry markers. If you put an initial on the heel, at least you can sort easily by person and then match up the socks not consumed by an appliance more quickly. This works on underwear too, if you mark it on the inside of the elastic waistband where no one will notice.

Another laundry-simplifying method is putting each person's laundry in a separate bin and letting each one put his own clothes away.

Bedtime Solutions

Establishing good sleep habits begins early in a child's life and is one of the best ways to improve the family's schedule. A book that helped immensely when my children were infants was *Solve Your Child's Sleep Problems* by Richard Ferber, M.D.,[2] which my pediatrician referred to me when my first child, Carolyn, was born. I learned the importance of sleep in my child's life and in mine, as well as methods for establishing a healthy bedtime and a way to enforce it (most of the time) by establishing a routine that was both enjoyable and relaxing for the child. That challenge increased as the children got older and could climb out of bed to ask for that fourteenth glass of water, but this book provided practical ways to handle many sleep-related problems of children. And once you're reasonably confident that you will have a calm, hassle-free bedtime, you're more likely to have some energy left for chores or bill-paying or a quiet cup of tea with your husband after everyone else is in bed.

Love in Writing

When my children were in elementary school, I packed their lunches. I didn't work outside our home at that time, and I had time to do that and also to write a brief note to each one every day. The note was just a word of encouragement, "I know you'll do great on your history test today," or affirmation, "I'm so proud of the way you sounded when you practiced the piano last night," or an expression of my love, "Remember that I love you very much today and every day." Sometimes I would include a Bible verse, especially one they were trying to memorize for Sunday school or Awana.

I didn't think the children really cared about the notes or noticed them—I even thought they might be embarrassed in front of their schoolmates, pulling out a little white 3-inch square note from their mom every day. But one day when I was rushed and didn't have time to include the notes, my son Andrew ran to the car after school (he was about seven at the time), and said, "What's wrong, Mom? Where was my note today?"

I saved the notes and stapled them together in little books called "Carolyn's First-Grade Notes" and so on, and today I'm extremely glad that I sent a bit of love with them every day to school.

Often busy schedules can crowd out time for loving communication. By making the most of small opportunities, like notes in lunch bags or left on a pillow before bedtime, busy moms can sneak in messages of love to their kids, messages that will be long remembered.

Safe at Home

When it is necessary and they are old enough to be home alone after school, be sure your children have everything they need to be safe and unafraid in your absence.

Of course, your telephone number is a must, along with numbers for people they could reach in an emergency, such as neighbors or relatives. It's a good idea for your child to call you at work to let you know he has arrived at home. Children must know how to call 911 and also understand what a true emergency is so that they don't call 911 when the Frisbee gets stuck in a tree. The children must know the rules on answering the door, and they must be sure to never tell a caller that their parents are not home. If you must have someone other than the usual driver or caregiver pick up your child from school, have a code word that the person must know in order for the child to go with him or her. Our code word was "Obadiah" (I don't remember how we came up with that), and we never had to use it. The children should also have change for making phone calls or a calling card they have practiced using.

Be sure to have healthy snacks available, as well as the materials each will need to do his homework. Instruct them in how to operate the microwave safely, never putting metal in it or leaving it unattended. Teach basic first aid skills and show the children where the first aid kit is kept. And discuss situations where he'll need to know what to do, like having friends over, losing the house key, or missing the bus.

Provide rules as to limitations on watching TV or playing video or computer games. Set up your computer so that they do not have unrestricted use to harmful websites, either with software or password protection so you must be there when they go online.

When you get home, take a few minutes to talk one-on-one with each child, asking specific questions about her day and showing your interest in her world. If the child answers in monosyllables or shakes of the head, ask what was his favorite part of the day, and what was the worst part of the day. Ask for one thing she can be thankful about today. Ask who she sat with at lunchtime or what new projects she's going to be working on.

Starting dinner or rushing around to put in laundry or do some other chore can wait until you have this important time of reconnection with your kids.

Time-Gobblers

Have you ever needed to be someplace in five or ten minutes and been unable to find your keys? I find this to be one of the most frustrating experiences I endure, so I hung one of those little key racks by the back door, and I plop the keys onto it as soon as I walk in. Of course, I still occasionally leave the keys in the keyhole and rush around frantically trying to find them before discovering this dangerous oversight.

Another time-waster for me is trying to find receipts, so now I keep them all in one folder, transferring them to my tax folder at the end of the year.

I even try to put my purse in one of two places, in the kitchen or my bedroom, so I don't have to spend time tracking it down when I'm ready to leave the house.

Pack a Picnic

Whether you're going across country or across town, packing your own food will save both money and time in your family's schedule. You won't have to stop at fast-food places or restaurants, and you can prepare more nutritious food at home anyway.

I like to take along sandwiches made with lunchmeat, preferably sliced turkey, roast beef, or ham, a slice of cheese, lettuce, and wheat bread, which my kids will actually eat if it's soft. They have never liked mayonnaise—which I love—so I leave the sandwiches dry. I usually include a bag of pretzels or chips and some washed, cut-up fruit like apples, oranges, or pears. Add some homemade or boxed cookies, and you have a great picnic lunch, eatable either at a picnic spot or in the car.

I always take along a plastic gallon bottle filled with water and quite a few plastic drinking cups since they have a way of getting stepped on, chewed on, or otherwise rendered unusable for the second drink. Even better are individual water bottles for everyone.

If it's a long trip, perishable foods can be stored in a cooler packed with ice. And be sure to include some wet wipe cloths for those sticky fingers.

Packing a picnic means that even if the "I'm hungry" chorus starts just as you pull out of your driveway, you're prepared.

Planning Ahead

I might as well admit it: I'm directionally impaired. That means I can get lost on the easiest, shortest trip, even right in my own town. If I come to an intersection and my gut feeling is that I should turn right to get to where I want to go, I know what I really must do is turn left. My driving instincts are poor to none. I inherited this inability from my mother, with whom I have driven hundreds of miles out of the way, missing the same exit three times on the way to visit my grandmother.

I bet you think I'm going to suggest getting one of those fancy cars with the computer systems that you tell where you want to go and the computer says aloud, "Turn left here, go three-quarters of a mile, and turn right." I can't afford one of those; but what I always do now is go to mapquest.com or another map site where I can type in my address and my destination, and it shows me a map and provides written driving directions as well. Occasionally I've found a few errors in the directions, but if I start out armed with one of these maps as well as a regular map or atlas, and I give myself plenty of extra time to get lost a few times, I can navigate to where I want to go with the best of 'em.

Staying Sane While Traveling

When my children were small, I kept a handwritten list of things to check off before I left the house and things to take on car trips of an hour or more in duration. Being sure the car had been serviced recently was one of the items to check off. On the household list were important tasks like checking to see that the coffeepot was turned off. I almost said being sure the iron was unplugged, but that is not a problem for me because I don't iron, preferring the fresh-from-the-dryer, not-too-wrinkled look.

Before taking a trip, I packed a shoebox for each child, keeping the boxes between trips and recycling or refreshing the contents. I've heard of mothers who use metal 9 x 13 pans with fitted plastic lids for their travel kits, one for each child. I included vacation bingo cards, something to draw on with a solid surface to support their paper, and crayons or washable markers. They also enjoyed sticking stickers onto paper when they were young, so I usually put some of those in, especially for my daughter. For very little money you can outfit a child's car activity box with fun items to occupy his attention.

I took food and candy for prizes for good behavior. My children enjoyed audio tapes in the car, and so did my husband and I. "Adventures in Odyssey" provided many hours of rapt travel listening for our family. And I led the children in games like spotting license plates from different states and finding letters on road signs.

I learned that a little preparation made car trips much more enjoyable for everyone.

Pooling Resources

Carpooling is an obvious and effective way to streamline your family's schedule and save time, gas money, and the stress of sitting in traffic. One mom I know calculated that every week she carpooled her children to their Christian school with another mother, she saved two and a half hours and about $10 in gasoline costs. That's about ten hours a month and $40, enough to have a family pizza night, rent a video, and still have money left over. And ten hours a month could be used for weekly lunches with friends or weekly volunteer efforts. Oh, okay, I guess it could also be used for housecleaning.

I used to drive every morning and another mom would bring the kids home after school, although this only works when they're very young and don't have after-school activities to consider. Sometimes driving both ways on certain days of the week works better, or even teaming up with two other moms if your child has a sports practice three times a week, especially if the practice location is some distance from your home.

Making the Most of Minutes

If your chauffeuring destination is somewhat distant and you have to go back and pick the kids up in an hour or two, say after sports practice, you often can drop them off and then do errands while they're practicing. You can usually find a grocery store nearby, and you can be all stocked up with food by the time practice is over. I started keeping my grocery store coupons in the car to be sure to have them handy when I did my shopping.

You might want to have a few healthy snacks ready when the children get into the car because they'll probably want something to eat once they discover that you've been to the store.

Who's Buying?

A mother with three young children in the grocery store suddenly noticed that her cart had some unexpected items in it, things she would never buy, like whopping boxes of candy. Knowing who the culprits had to be, she pointed to the items and asked which child had brought his money in order to buy the candy pile. The children exchanged glances and began taking the sweets out of the cart and putting them back on the shelf, not in the right places, of course. I guess that mother made her point: Don't load up the grocery cart if you can't pay the bill.

If possible, go to the grocery store without the little darlings. Go at off times, even before the kids get up or after they're in bed, if you're not too tired by then. Avoid going on the way home from work and Saturday morning, if you can. Be sure to have a list and stick to it.

Grandparents' Day

Don't forget to thank grandparents, aunts and uncles, neighbors, and whoever else helps you with your kids. I've noticed that grandparents often pour much of their time and energy into their grandchildren, partly because they love the kids, but also because of necessity when the parents or single moms work.

Working schedules often don't coincide exactly with school schedules, not to mention summer vacation time, and it's often the grandparents who make it all work by driving children to and from school and taking them to doctor and dentist appointments, music lessons, and sports practices. They often prepare their lunches and help with homework, and even take them shopping for necessities if a parent is struggling financially.

What would we do without grandparents and other extended family who help us raise our children?

My mother took care of my daughter so my husband and I could go on a business trip years ago, and while I was semifrantic the whole time because I had never been away from my baby before, it was a good break for us. Mother was always willing to babysit, and I tried not to overuse her, but it's so comforting knowing your child is with a loving grandparent or other relative.

Why not have a "Thank you, Grandma" party where Grandma gets the You Are Special plate, her favorite food is served, and you and your children write her a letter expressing specifically how much she means to you. Tell her that without her help you don't know how you could even work to support your family.

The smile you'll see on her face will let you know how important it is to remember to value and appreciate those who do so much for us quietly and consistently, year in and year out.

Special Sitters

When my daughter was a baby, I was your typical mother of a firstborn. We had tried to have a baby for several years, and I was 35 by the time Carolyn was born. I adored her, and I had probably a too-high fear level about leaving her in anyone else's care. Though my mother often babysat for us (I figured that since she had raised four children successfully to adulthood, she knew what she was doing), there were times when Mother was unavailable and my husband had a business dinner we needed to attend.

I geared up for days for the first time I hired a babysitter, writing down every possible instruction and precaution, making elaborate telephone lists of whom to call if she needed help. I asked neighbors for recommendations on sitters and settled on Stephanie, an eighth-grade girl who was the oldest of five children. She was experienced with babies, but not old enough to be talking on the phone to boys while she was supposed to be taking care of my darling. I invited Stephanie over to meet us and get to know my Carolyn before the actual night she was to babysit. And I experienced quite a bit of apprehension while we were out, only to find everything peaceful at home, Carolyn asleep, and Stephanie reading a book when we returned.

We were fortunate to build a relationship with Stephanie, and Carolyn called her "Fuffie." She continued to babysit for us until we moved away three years later.

If you can develop a good relationship with a sitter, it will help your child feel comfortable and safe when the sitter is taking care of him. Having the continuity of the same caregiver builds security for the child. And it builds a relationship among you, your sitter, and your child. Fuffie cried when we moved, and we did too.

One thing that will make family scheduling easier is having reliable and trustworthy child care from someone your child enjoys. While you don't have to be as fearful as I was as a first-time mother, finding the right person and building that relationship will provide great benefits to you and your child.

Family Meeting

Family meetings should be fun so the kids don't dread them for days in advance. Be sure everyone is involved and make the meeting short. It could be divided into two simple segments: Concerns and Plans. Anyone is free to raise a concern that is then to be discussed freely. Anything can be said as long as it's done with respect and kindness. You might want to put a tentative time limit on each topic of say, 15 minutes, and at the end, if everyone has had a chance to comment, try to come to a consensus that fits within your family standards. Just remember, you are the adult and the parent, and the buck stops with you.

And make the main point of the meeting planning a fun family event that never gets canceled so that your family is sure to have at least one night a week where everyone does something together, even if it's just a favorite TV show or a one-hour board game.

Inexpensive fun family activities:

✳ Take a walk.

✳ Go inline skating (those without skates can walk or ride bikes).

✳ Visit the library and borrow a video.

✳ Make cookies.

✳ Go on a picnic, even in the backyard.

✳ Help an elderly neighbor or family member cut grass or shovel snow.

✳ Play a board or card game or even tic-tac-toe.

✳ Schedule a family meeting night to plan and choose upcoming activities.

✳ Attend a free concert in the park.

Being There for Them

I know several couples who juggle their schedules in order to have one of the parents home with the children as much as possible. Annette has arranged for flextime at her office so that she can start early and get off in time to pick up her son from school on days when her husband, Ed, who often works during the evenings, can't pick him up. My friend Linda works at home three days a week as a book editor, and she is there when her children come home from school most days, making arrangements for their care two days of the week.

Bob has a consulting business he conducts from home, so he is usually available when the children are at home and his wife, Maggie, is at work. Sarah and Tom are both teachers, and they stagger their schedules so that one of them comes home each day when the children do.

Creativity isn't always enough to allow a parent to be with a child most of the time, but you'll be surprised at the innovative solutions you can come up with, and what your employer will agree to, if you brainstorm about ways to have at least one parent with the children as much as possible.

Working Later

This is another obvious idea, but doing your housework after the children are in bed when they're small really helps. When they're up and on the go, it's wonderful to spend time with them rather than having to work every minute.

I remember enjoying just sitting or lying on the floor when my children were small and watching them discover and wonder and learn. I spent a lot of time reading books to them and playing simple games, but just being there with them was something I enjoyed then and look back on now with happiness and satisfaction.

While I was pretty tired by the time I put them to bed at night, I often saved laundry or dishes to do once they were asleep, freeing myself up for time to just enjoy my little kids for that brief time when they were small.

Things you can do the night before:

Put the Crock-Pot on the countertop to remind you to start dinner before heading off for the day.

Make a quick checklist of errands for the next day so you don't have to worry that you're forgetting something in the morning.

Do all the things the kids are doing: make your lunch, lay out your clothes, pack up your briefcase.

Overscheduling

A little girl in my children's school had leukemia. Her mother called me to ask if I could pick up her older girl and drive her to school one day since the mother would be at the hospital that morning. They lived about three blocks away. I said I'd be glad to pick up Kristen at 8:30 for school.

I hung up, pleased that Joanne had called on me. I wrote it on my calendar. I was taking college courses at the time, and it was finals week. From my track record, I knew I could forget to pick up Kristen, so I wrote myself a note the night before and put it on the kitchen counter: GET KRISTEN.

By now you probably know that I forgot to pick her up. In fact, I went to my final exam that morning after dropping my kids off at school, and I never even realized I had forgotten Kristen until after lunch!

When it dawned on me, I frantically called the school and called Joanne in case she was home from the hospital by then. She was gracious and said she had called someone else to get Kristen when I didn't show up. I felt awful—just what that poor woman needs: a sick child *and* an unreliable neighbor!

I learned that even the biggest notes and the best intentions don't always work on superbusy days. I probably should have realized that with the children's schedule and my final exams, taking on one more morning responsibility would not have worked. I should have said that word which is so hard and foreign to me, *no*, saving everyone involved a lot of grief.

Too Many Good Things?

Jackie's elementary-school-age son and daughter were active in sports and activities, which is good. Jason was in youth hockey through their town's park district. He was also on his school soccer team and went to Awana every

Wednesday night at church. Jorie was in her third year of piano lessons, and her teacher told Jackie that her daughter had real ability, which of course delighted her parents. She had also shown artistic ability in her painting class, and her parents wanted to do everything they could do to develop her fine arts talents. Jorie was on a community traveling swim team, and she, too, attended Awana on Wednesdays. Both children went to friends' birthday parties and got together with fellow students to complete projects.

Needless to say, Jackie and her husband, John, spent countless hours in the car chauffeuring the children to the beneficial activities they participated in. John also served as a coach for Jason's hockey team. Jackie was room mother for one of the children each year, alternating between the two to be totally fair. Because she was a stay-at-home mom, she sensed an expectation from other moms and from the teacher that she should drive on every field trip since they assumed she had the time.

When Jackie's mother had a stroke and needed rehab in a nursing home, Jackie and John knew that something had to give.

They decided that at least while Grandma was sick, each child would participate in one activity each season plus Awana. Jorie continued piano lessons, but put her painting class on hold. Jason chose hockey over soccer. Jackie said she would be unable to drive on field trips until her mother was out of rehab.

The choices were hard ones, but the family gained a bit of breathing room by scaling back on activities that were good and beneficial, but which pulled them all in too many directions at once.

❦ ❦ ❦

Only on Thursdays...

I used to think doing certain chores on certain days of the week, or even serving the same dish; for example, spaghetti on Monday, was far too limiting and structured for my creative, free-thinking spirit. But I no longer think that way.

Some of the most organized and productive women I know have certain days every week for laundry, other designated days for meal-planning and grocery shopping, and set days for doing errands.

By limiting laundry to Thursdays, everyone in the family knows he'd better get that favorite T-shirt into the hamper by Wednesday night or live without it for another week. And everyone will have clean clothes for the weekend and for church.

Here's one idea for planning your week. Just plug in what works best for you:

Sunday—Church followed by a day off. I sure wish I followed God's instructions for taking the Sabbath rest, but I often treat it like any other day, and after church I rush around, working.

Monday—Bill paying or other paperwork, including to-do list for the week.

Tuesday—One hour of cleaning.

Wednesday—Another hour of cleaning.

Thursday—Laundry (kids can put away their own at a very young age).

Friday—Grocery list and grocery shop.

Saturday—Errands and catch-up.

The Trusty Timer

Sometimes getting a child to clean his room is more difficult than going in yourself and cleaning like a whirling dervish until the job is done. When my daughter was preschool age, I'd go in and say I was "helping" her, and what happened was that I cleaned, sorted, and threw away old gum wrappers and other trash while she sat beside me playing happily. She was supposed to be doing her part; for instance, picking up all of her marbles and putting them into a little pouch, or putting all the crayons into a box. But she'd put a couple of marbles in and then start making a little bird out of a tissue or some other craft she seemed to be able to do with even an old shoelace.

Finally, I realized I was doing the cleaning while she played. So we started the 15-minute system. I brought a timer up to her room and set it for 15 minutes. We cleaned together for the first 15 minutes, and I reset the timer and left her in the room for the next 15 with a measurable goal, say, a three-foot square on the carpeting that was to be cleared of all debris and toys. If she accomplished her goal, I worked with her for the next 15 minutes, and so on. By alternating 15-minute segments, we eventually made some progress.

From Sink to Table

I don't own a dishwasher. When I moved into this house, there was no dishwasher, so I put "get dishwasher" on my to-do list, along with other "gets" like "get new furnace," "get new garage door opener," and "get new water softener." As soon as I moved in I purchased the new furnace, along with a new air conditioner, and I had the garage door opener refurbished. But I just never got around to the dishwasher. I probably would have by now if there had been an old dishwasher in place, but getting one would mean having a cabinet torn out and lots of carpentry work done. And I have filled all the kitchen cabinets to capacity.

So we've become used to washing the dishes by hand, and it really isn't so bad. One thing we do is dry the dishes and, instead of putting them back in the cabinet, we set the table for the next meal. I used to do this even when I had a dishwasher, and it really simplifies mealtime, helping the family schedule to progress a little more smoothly.

Saving Trips

Like many parents, when my children were toddlers, I taught them to scoot down the stairs on their tummies (feet first) so they didn't fall coming down the traditional grown-up way. My boys took great delight in doing this even when they were old enough to walk down. When Andrew was five he went down, face and tummy toward the stairs, and he scraped a little red spot right in the middle of his forehead because it rubbed the same place on each carpeted step. I guess it didn't hurt at first because three-year-old Steve had to have one just like it on his forehead, so he did the same thing. Only later did they complain about their foreheads hurting because of the rug burns on their poor little faces.

But speaking of stairs, I save myself trips by leaving things that need to go upstairs at the foot of the stairs for my next trip, and vice versa at the top of the stairs. Of course, this method can get out of hand if I fold laundry and pile it all up at the bottom of the stairs, waiting to go up and blocking everybody's access to the stairs. But within reason, it works very well.

Making a Date

I'm trying to get used to using one of those fancy notebook/planner things that everyone carries around now, at least everyone who doesn't have a handheld electronic scheduler. But what I still like best—and always will—is the old-fashioned large wall calendar. I excitedly purchase mine every December. I like the plain ones that cost about $10 or $12 and have a whole month on each page. First I copy everyone's birthday from the old calendar onto the new, adding another year to each age (except for my own birthday, which remains ageless but dutifully noted on the calendar in case anyone forgets and needs to be sure exactly when it is).

If you hang your calendar in the busiest room of your house—the kitchen in mine—and somehow attach a pencil on a string, you can encourage everyone to immediately write a plan or commitment on the main family calendar when the commitment is made (after asking Mom and Dad first). If it's written down immediately, there's much less chance of forgetting to make a note of it and missing the occasion.

Just plan on replacing the pencil frequently because they really do sprout legs, walk away, and hide, so that whenever you want one they're nowhere in sight.

Family activities that can burn about 250 calories in an hour:

  ★ Bowling

  ★ Bicycling

  ★ Dancing

  ★ Ice skating

  ★ Playing Frisbee

  ★ Raking and Weeding

Planning to Plan

I'm still learning that I need to take a calendar everywhere I go. What would really work best for me would be to fold up my big kitchen calendar and stuff it into my purse because that has all the family's plans, as well as birthdays and special occasions, on it. But since that doesn't work, and since I often need to check the calendar when I'm nowhere near the wall calendar at home, I've accepted the fact that I must carry one in my purse. Of course, entering things on both my purse calendar and then on the kitchen calendar is hard to remember, but as I said, I'm training myself that both entries must be made.

I even have one of those lovely planner-type zipper binders, too big for my purse, but covered with a beautiful tapestry-like fabric. I can take notes in it besides writing down future dates while I'm away from home. It has a section for phone numbers, and because I figure this is about as close as I'm ever going to get to a handheld electronic device, I'm determined to successfully use my planner. In fact, I plan to have mastered my planner by this time next year.

Washing Up

Streamlining the family's schedule must include kitchen activities. When I'm doing things efficiently, I wash fruits and vegetables as soon as I get home from the grocery store, storing them in plastic containers or plastic bags in the refrigerator. It's so nice to go to the refrigerator at mealtime and find already prepared ingredients to work with in creating a meal. And having celery sticks ready for snacking, along with a big jar of peanut butter for dipping, makes the kids more likely to choose a healthy snack. If you don't have a lettuce storage container, you can put a folded paper towel in the bottom of a plastic bag before putting your washed head of lettuce in it.

Fungus with a Purpose

One Christmas I sent my cousin Laura in Nashville a kit with which you can grow your own Shitake mushrooms. Laura is a fabulous cook who creates the most complicated and delicious foods, seemingly with no effort at all, so I knew she would be able to make good use of this living gift. She is as calm as she can be, even with three little girls running around the kitchen while she chops and mixes and bakes and grates. Laura seems unruffled, no matter how many people are in her house.

The kit was supposed to be placed in an area with humidity to encourage the mushrooms to grow, so Laura put it in the bathroom on one of the corners of the bathtub in its little box with the lid off. One of her friends came over, and after using the bathroom, asked if she didn't think it was time to clean the tub since things had started growing on it!

So beware of what's growing in your bathroom.

Laura streamlines her Christmas schedule by beginning in November to make and freeze dozens of pound cakes and other goodies to give later for Christmas gifts. Between homeschooling three little girls and being a social butterfly herself, Laura needs to organize and prepare in advance for her holiday baking extravaganza. She and her eight-year-old daughter, Lily, have even won prizes for their baking prowess.

Keep It Simple, Sweetheart

Saving Money in Unexpected Places

%% %% %%

When I went from relative riches-to-rags after my divorce several years ago, I found myself needing to rebuild my finances from almost nothing. Suddenly, saving money and being frugal took on a whole new meaning for me. While I dreaded starting over from scratch, the things I have learned since then have convinced me that finding bargains and living simply can actually be fun. As I began shopping in resale stores and reading newsletters like the *Tightwad Gazette,* I was amazed to find that you can almost make a game of saving money.

My friend Gretchen found a navy blue overstuffed loveseat for $25 at a neighborhood resale shop. She disliked the fabric it was upholstered with because it didn't match the rest of her furniture. This amazing woman decided she would reupholster the sofa herself and began by removing one piece of fabric at a time, making a duplicate of that piece in the fabric she had chosen, and stapling or sewing it back onto the loveseat. After several days of challenging work, Gretchen had a new-looking sofa in green-and-white-plaid fabric.

While I don't have her sewing abilities and am sure a sofa I had re-covered would need to be put out at the curb with the garbage, I have had my own small money-saving victories. Like the time I found three new-looking hard cover books at a garage sale for 50 cents each, carved out a rectangular shape from all the pages using a disposable razor blade tool, and gave each child his own book safe for Christmas. I had seen them offered on the Internet for $25!

In this chapter we're going to explore money-saving techniques, and we're going to start looking at saving money as a recreational activity. You can even give yourself a little prize when you manage to find an especially good bargain, maybe a tall regular coffee at Starbuck's, not the exotic and more expensive large, flavored ones.

Grab your treasure-hunting gear, and let's save some money!

I Think I Can

I'm not real handy. A room I wallpapered looks as though it were undertaken as a kindergarten class art project. Lumps and cracks and tilting patterns abound, but hey, I did it and I'm proud of it. I overlook the gaps and bumps, and it's fine.

When my children were in early elementary school and we would attend a birthday party, the mothers always said, "Oh, it's so nice that you let your child use her creativity by wrapping the packages for you." I smiled kindly at them and said, "Actually, *I* wrapped the packages. My children could have done a much better job than *that*."

But when I bought my house and the indoor porch floor consisted of concrete covered with old and lumpy green indoor-outdoor carpeting, I decided it couldn't look much worse if I tackled tiling it myself.

Laying ceramic tile was quite an adventure, but I got it done. It took me days to do and many trips to Home Depot to rent wet saws and then take them back when they broke. Each time I had to have a friend help me unload the heavy wet saw from the back of my mini van and onto the porch. I also took a how-to class at a tile store, watched for the tile I wanted to go on sale, and barreled ahead into a daunting project that became one of the most satisfying things I've ever done. I even tiled the stairs! I saved close to $2000 on this project. By now everyone I know is tired of my saying I did the tile myself whenever we're on the porch, but I really am proud of it.

And it looks better than one of my wallpapering or gift-wrapping jobs.

> One only needs two tools in life:
> WD-40 to make things go, and duct
> tape to make them stop.
> —G. M. WEILACHER

Do-It-Myself

When I called my neighbor Shirley, she said she was installing a new thermostat. I was so impressed, and I asked her how she had learned to do it. She said she read some materials she got at a home improvement store and just tackled it all by herself. I said I'd pray that she wouldn't get electrocuted and hung up.

The next time I saw her, I asked her how it had turned out, and she said fine. I then asked if she was now going out to clear the back 40 (an old farm term I heard my dad use), and she said that, in fact, she was just about to start trimming her trees. It really is amazing what we can do when we believe we can.

Discovering that she does all these complicated things herself inspired me to not only read a pruning book and start trimming my own trees (the ones I could reach), but I also attended a Faux Finishing class at a local home improvement store and painted an old hutch cabinet in my kitchen with several layers of green and white paint mixed with glaze. I get a lot of compliments on the finished piece, but to me it will always look like a giant, pale green Frango Mint from Marshall Field's.

Realizing that I can tackle a new job myself—and gaining the confidence to try—has saved me considerable money.

Do-it-yourself money savers:

- ✶ Make your lunch and take it to work instead of eating out.

- ✶ Wash and iron dress shirts and blouses instead of sending them to the laundry.

- ✶ Dry-clean clothes in your dryer with a dry-cleaning kit purchased at the grocery store.

- ✶ Make your own play dough by mixing in a saucepan 2 cups flour, 1 cup salt, 2 cups water, 4 teaspoons cream of tartar, 2 tablespoons oil, and food coloring to desired color. Cook until it pulls away from the pan. Knead as it cools.

- ✶ Wash and chop your own salad ingredients instead of buying the ready-to-eat bagged variety.

- ✶ Give homemade gifts like bread, jelly, cakes, cookies, or fudge.

- ✶ Grow some of your vegetables and herbs in your garden.

Selling by Owner

When I sold my house, I was determined to at least try to sell it myself. It had been appraised recently when I was considering using a Realtor, and I kept my eye on what comparable houses were going for. I had everything repaired, and I repainted where necessary, and one spring day I planted my For Sale by Owner sign out in the front yard and up at the corner of our street as well.

It took four months and many showings, but finally a lovely couple who were moving back here from living in Jerusalem as teachers for the last 30 years bought it at my asking price, which was a shock and a very rare occurrence. We wound up becoming friends, and I left feeling that the house was in good hands. I've even been back inside it since then when they invited me in to see their changes, which was both enjoyable and emotionally hard at the same time.

For several months after I moved I dreamed that I was back in my kitchen and the children were playing around on the kitchen floor, when suddenly the new owners came in and I realized I was in someone else's house!

Even Your Hairdresser Won't Know

After I started going gray and before I started going broke, I used to get my hair done every six weeks. I enjoyed seeing Kim, my hairdresser, and I loved the way she cut and colored my hair.

But as my financial situation changed, I worried about how I could keep going to Kim for my hair color and cuts because it was $60 each time I went. I knew if I tried doing my own color, I'd wind up looking like a too-old-to-pull-it-off teen wannabe with four different hair colors.

When I couldn't maintain my Kim luxury any longer, I prepared to tell her I had to stop getting her gorgeous color. I thought I could continue with the haircuts, but I'd have to do the coloring myself. But at my next appointment before I could tell her, she said, "I hate to tell you this, but the chemicals in the hair dyes are making me sick, so I'm going to have to stop coloring. I'll help you figure out how to buy the colors you need and mix them to look like the color I do. Then you can just come to me for your haircuts, which are only $20."

Today I have hair color I can afford, and it's all the same color!

Taking My Time

The couple who sold me my present home had lived in it for 39 years and raised their four children here. Paul told me how he had painstakingly done a lot of the fine work on the house himself, even though by day he was a college professor. When they had bought the house, its siding was painted dark brown and was peeling. Paul spent two years removing all the brown paint with a heat gun and a scraper, and then he repainted the house white, which it remains today. Thanks to his effort, the house still has its original siding—in very good shape.

He said something that I've remembered and almost chanted to myself when my frustration mounts and I feel like hurrying to get a job done. He said, "I just take my time and try to do it right." Now I try to slow myself down and take off the pressure by remembering that Paul spent two years making the outside of my house look beautiful. I really don't need to rush on whatever job I'm doing. Instead, I want to take my time and do it right.

E-mailing Uncle Sam

When I was married, my husband and I had a tax pre-parer. I gathered up all our receipts and documents, sorted them out, gave them to him, and *voilà!* He presented us with tax returns to sign, write a check for, and send in to the IRS.

After my divorce my returns were much less complicated (much less income!), but I still thought I needed an accoun-tant to prepare them. Finally, I worked up my courage and started using tax preparation software and filing electroni-cally. My returns really are rather simple, and the program walks me through the forms, asking necessary questions along the way.

I now save hundreds of dollars each year by doing my taxes myself. And if I'm getting a refund, it comes within days.

Glue Gun Adventures

One of my jobs at my children's school was to organize our Spring Salad Supper event for all the school moms. It occurred during my "crafty" craze when I loved to make wreaths and swags and anything with dried or silk flowers.

I decided to make small wreaths that could double as candleholders out of dried orange slices, figuring they would be fragrant and pretty at the same time. I had a small food dehydrating machine, and I would slice up a couple of oranges, spread them on the shelves in the dehydrator, and remove them the next day when they were nice and dry. This process took months because I had to make about 25 wreaths by gluing the oranges slices together in layers with my hot glue gun and decorating them with bittersweet berries and raffia ribbon.

The custom was to sell the centerpieces at the end of the salad supper, and all the wreaths sold except for three, which I kept for myself and hung on our vacation home wall.

We didn't visit the vacation home for more than a month that year, and the next time we walked into the house, it was swarming with moths that had somehow hatched from little bugs that had developed in the orange-slice wreaths.

Imagine my horror when I had to go back and call all the women who had purchased the wreaths and warn them of impending infestations.

That experience did much to dampen my craftiness, but I did make my children's Halloween costumes that year out of furry fabric remnants hot glued together into a black panther, a tiger, and a lion, created for a few dollars in a few minutes.

Paying as I Go

We all know that using a credit card is really taking out a loan for something that may be long gone when the time to pay up comes. I hate getting a credit card statement that includes food I ate weeks ago at a restaurant. Even those new clothes at such good prices look somewhat dingy when I glance up from that credit card bill.

I try very hard to pay off my balance each month so I don't incur interest charges, but there are times, such as Christmas, when I don't manage to do it.

After shopping around for the best deal on a credit card (no annual fee and a lower rate of interest than other cards), I opened a new account after my divorce. I was charged a higher interest rate at first because my credit rating had been shredded along with my affluent lifestyle. But after several years of prompt payments under my belt, I called the company and asked what the lowest rate they could give me would be. They dropped the rate by two full percentage points and agreed to give me the lower rate permanently because I had been a good customer.

I still try to pay off my balance each month, but when I'm not able to, I am somewhat comforted by the fact that I have obtained the best credit card deal I could.

When Fewer Is Better

Most people get offer after offer for "preapproved" credit cards, bearing high interest rates, of course, which are not usually heralded like the benefits of having the new card.

But the more credit cards you have, the harder it is to keep them organized, check statements, and study them for tax deductions at the end of the year. Multiple cards make it easier to charge up balances, and many also have an annual fee. Plus, the more statements you have each month, the longer it takes to pay your bills, so I have reduced mine to two no-annual-fee cards after calling to get the lowest possible

interest rates. I ignore other offers, shredding them because
of horror stories about identity theft and other crimes made
easier by someone being able to access this type of mail.

Thanks, but No Thanks

Financial "offers" I always avoid include credit disability
insurance where the creditor will pay off my credit cards or
my mortgage in case I die, and long service contracts on
appliances or electronic equipment. Often term life insurance is a more economical way to cover debts in the event
of death, and one of my rules is to keep credit cards paid off
anyway, as much as I can. When I am offered a service contract or credit insurance, I always turn it down, preferring to
"self-insure" and cover these losses myself.

Another automatic "no" for me is book, CD, and record
clubs. Unbeknownst to me, my daughter signed up for a CD
club when she was 12, and it took me four months of letters
and phone calls to get the company to stop harassing her.
They sent some CDs automatically and then we had the
additional struggle of having to return them and get the company to cancel the bill.

Sometimes these "helpful" or "free" offers turn out to be
costly indeed. I read carefully before signing up for credit
protection, service contracts, or purchasing clubs and make
a habit of resisting the urge to say yes.

The World of Work

An important part of money management is educating our children about the subject. Although I was a stay-at-home mom for my children's elementary and middle school years, once I started working, I enjoyed showing my children the work I did. One way to do that was to participate in "take your child to work" or "job shadowing" day. This is a great way to introduce your child to the world of work outside the home, not that they don't see moms and dads working around the house day in and day out.

Getting a glimpse of a parent doing the job he is paid to do can be eye-opening for kids. I took my son Steve to work with me last year, and he enjoyed the day. My company encourages participation in the annual job-shadowing day, and I let him answer my phone and send out e-mails for me. I later found several surprise postings on my electronic calendar, like "Make a chocolate cake today."

Steve attended meetings with me, and I could tell he had had his fill of talk when his fingers began drumming on the table like a big spider flexing its muscles. He didn't even realize he was doing it, but one of the others at the meeting laughed and said, "I guess Steve thinks this meeting has gone on long enough," to which he eagerly nodded and smiled.

Letting your child experience your job is a good way to get him thinking about what types of work he does and doesn't like, what interests him and what doesn't, and how much effort goes into earning the money to support the family.

And Steve couldn't wait to come to job-shadowing day the next year.

❀   ❀   ❀

Ways to supplement your income:*

* ✷ Moonlight—whatever you do during the day, you can let people know that you do side work as well. Many people will be eager to use your services, especially if they are a little lower-priced than they would pay elsewhere.

* ✷ Freelance—similar to moonlighting.

* ✷ Be an election judge.

* ✷ Monitor testing at schools and universities in your area.

* ✷ Seasonal part-time work at stores.

* ✷ House sit and pet sit.

* ✷ Be careful on pyramid and work-at-home schemes. If they ask you to send in even $1, it's probably just a way for the promoters to make money, not a way for YOU to make money.

* ✷ Home party sales.

* ✷ Substitute teaching.

* ✷ Sign up with a temp agency—you can accept or reject assignments according to your schedule.

* ✷ Telemarketing.

* ✷ Work overtime.

* ✷ Sell used books on Amazon.com and other items on ebay.com.

* If you're married and/or have children at home, think and pray carefully before embarking on one of these ways to earn extra money. Your family and your health must come first, even if you really could use some extra cash.

Check, Charge, or Cash?

I took my credit card out of my purse and put it away safely at home so I wouldn't charge anything, but I forgot that I had taken this prudent financial measure when I invited my 17-year-old daughter to go out to dinner with me one evening.

We enjoyed our meal of artichoke and spinach dip with Portobello mushrooms and salad. When the check arrived, I headed for my trusty credit card and quickly remembered my stop-charging technique of removing the card from my purse.

I usually carry very little cash, so the $8 I had was considerably shy of covering our $19 bill (plus tip). Embarrassed, I considered using my debit card before realizing its balance was $4. I started writing a check on another account containing $59 when the waiter approached. He said, "I'm sorry, but I wanted to save you the trouble of writing a check because we don't take them." He walked away and I asked my daughter how she felt about washing dishes for our dinner.

"This is no problem, Mom. Write me a check, I'll go cash it, and we'll be fine," which she did as I sat at the table thinking of how brilliantly I'd avoided charging our dinner on my credit card.

The moral of this story: Be sure you never pull a stunt like this accompanied by a child who's not old enough to drive yet. I now carry a credit card, just in case.

❧   ❧   ❧

> Give all your worries and cares to God, for he cares about what happens to you.
> —1 PETER 5:7 NLT

Gifts Galore

I'm sort of bragging here, but I have about 50 people on my Christmas list. My list includes friends, friends' children, relatives of all ages, neighbors, and, of course, my own children. I also give quite a few birthday gifts. Buying gifts for 50 people makes me feel like a tiny chickadee who has volunteered to build a nest for an eagle: Where and how am I going to gather all the individual sticks and twigs I'll need and transport them to this gigantic nest? But with a little planning, I'm able to pick up gifts here and there and slowly build my Christmas gift supply.

I shop after Christmas for the next year, not right after Christmas, but by about the third week in January when things are really cheap. This year I bought sweaters in various colors and sizes for my friends: They started out at $59 and were reduced to $40 right before Christmas. Right after Christmas they went on sale for $25, and I bought them when they were 50 percent off that sale price.

Baskets also make good gifts. I have a bunch of baskets I have acquired over the years in my attic. One year I put jars of spaghetti sauce and packages of spaghetti in baskets for an instant meal. There are endless varieties on homemade gift baskets: corn muffin mix and an inexpensive muffin tin, a jelly assortment, or dried bean soups.

Mugs also make good gifts: mugs containing teabags, cocoa mix, or a delicious coffee.

But you can't beat the price of gift coupons. I always ask my children to give me hairbrushing coupons ("I promise to brush Mom's hair for ten minutes") because that is one of my favorite treats. Or a car washing coupon where the child will wash my car without nagging or payment. Kids can give each other coupons for chores to be done for each other as well as babysitting coupons to aunts and uncles with young children.

> God has given gifts to each of you from his variety of spiritual gifts. Manage them well so that God's generosity can flow through you.
> —1 Peter 4:10 NLT

More Favorite (Cheap) Gifts

Homemade goodies aren't always economical, even though they are delicious. By the time you purchase the nuts and chocolate for a batch of fudge, you could have purchased a nice gift and saved yourself the time and effort in cooking.

But I have found a few standbys that are both affordable and popular. The key is in economies of scale. Make a quadruple batch and then cut and package them with colorful plastic wrap on holiday paper plates (also purchased after Christmas last year), and stick on a gift tag and bow. The recipes on these pages work well for gifts. The only hard part will be keeping the kids (and yourself, if you're tempted the way I am) from devouring the gifts before they can be delivered.

Delicious Cookies

1 can sweetened condensed milk (you can use fat-free, if you like)
6 ounces semisweet chocolate chips
20 graham crackers
salt
nonstick spray

Pulverize graham crackers and then mix with condensed milk, chocolate chips, and a dash of salt. Spray cookie sheet with nonstick spray. Spoon mixture onto sheet and bake at 350° for 10 minutes. Remove from sheet immediately.

Laura's Eggnog Pound Cake

1 stick butter, softened
1 stick margarine, softened
½ cup shortening
6 eggs
1 teaspoon vanilla extract
½ teaspoon coconut extract
3 cups flour
3 cups sugar
1 cup eggnog
1 teaspoon lemon extract
½ cup coconut

Cream together butter, margarine, shortening, and sugar. Add eggs one at a time, beating well. Add eggnog, vanilla, lemon, and coconut extracts, and then flour. Stir in coconut. Bake in 2 greased and floured loaf pans at 325° for 1 hour and 15 minutes.

Haystacks

6 ounces semisweet chocolate chips
6 ounces butterscotch chips
4 teaspoons oil
4 cups chow mein noodles
4 cups miniature marshmallows

Melt together chocolate chips and butterscotch chips. Add oil. In large bowl mix chow mein noodles and miniature marshmallows. Pour melted chocolate mixture over and stir thoroughly. Drop by spoonfuls on a waxed-paper lined cookie sheet. Chill.

Shortbread

1 cup butter
½ cup sugar
1½ cups flour

Cream together butter and sugar. Stir in flour. Chill. On floured board, roll half of dough to one-quarter to one-half inch thick. Cut into bars 2 x 1 inches. Bake on ungreased cookie sheet at 300° for 30 minutes. Cool slightly before removing from cookie sheet.

Homemade Heirlooms

My friend Carrie's extended family has created a clever Christmas gift solution. Each of the 16 adults in the group draws a name and gives a gift to only one adult. Everyone still gives modest gifts to the 12 children in the group, but each person only gives a gift to one adult. To make it even better, each adult must make the gift given to the adult—men and women alike create their own gifts, and everyone has begun to look forward eagerly to who will have his or her name and what will be made as a gift.

The men have made birdhouses, picture frames, homemade spaghetti sauce, and coupons for two hours of computer instruction time, household repairs, or babysitting. They have assembled tool kits, emergency auto kits with flares, blankets, and a battery-powered light, or the beans and seasonings for homemade soup.

The women have knitted or crocheted afghans, made wreaths or topiaries with materials purchased from a craft store, baked bread or cookies, painted a craft store serving tray, and gathered a bulb assortment with a promise to plant them at the right time.

Often the stories that go with how the gift was made are even better than the gift.

Teaming Up to Save

My sister-in-law Cindy can squeeze more out of a dollar than anyone else I know. I learned one of her secrets when

I asked her how she can be so generous with the children in our extended family every Christmas.

She told me that she started a bank account with her father as the cosigner, and the account requires both signatures on checks. She deposits a modest amount of money into the account every payday. She instructed her dad not to let her give him any sob stories about how she needed to access the account in the middle of the summer or any other time, but instead to insist she not touch the money until November, when each year she finds that she has a nice little Christmas fund built up.

Gaining on Debt

If you pay half your mortgage payment every two weeks instead of paying the entire amount once a month, you will make one additional mortgage payment each year, reducing the length of your mortgage by as much as several years, depending on the term of your loan. And if you can add a little bit extra to your payments—being sure to indicate on your check and the mortgage statement that you want the extra applied to reducing your loan's principal—you can pay it off even sooner and increase the equity in your home. For example, if you add $83 to your $1000 monthly mortgage payment, your 30-year loan will be paid off six years early.

Another way to save is to keep an eye on interest rates and check every few months to see if you should refinance your mortgage at a lower interest rate than you presently have. And if you put less than a 20 percent down payment on your home when you purchased it, keep track of your remaining principal due and ask to have the private mortgage insurance (PMI) dropped when you reach 20 percent. Sometimes by getting an appraisal, if the value of the house has increased, you can have the PMI eliminated because you now have 20 percent equity or more because of the increase in value.

Write on Time

I keep all my bills that need paying in a certain spot right by my computer monitor. One thing that helped me establish the habit of being sure to pay my bills twice a month was to write which bills were due when on my calendar. After I paid them, I'd scratch them off on the calendar and enter the same bill on the same day next month on the calendar.

Making sure your bills are paid on time not only protects your credit rating—it also prevents late charges from being assessed to your account.

Mistakes Happen

It's important to check your bills for accuracy or errors as soon as the bills arrive. If you find a charge you didn't make, call the company right away. If you are told they will investigate the charge, mark on your calendar when they said they should have an answer, and call again if you haven't heard. Then check the next bill to be sure the error has been corrected. If a company refuses to correct your bill, don't give up. Send a letter to the chief executive officer, telling him or her of your experience and explaining that you are canceling your account (unless it's the one and only electric company in your town).

If you still get no results on an erroneous bill, contact the Better Business Bureau in your area.

A Dollar Saved

I've found that money I never see is easier to save. In addition to a retirement savings program at work, I have a money market account for real estate taxes. I divided up the annual tax bill by twelve and that amount is automatically deposited from my checking account into the money market account each month, so that when tax time comes around, I don't have to find that big chunk. And I get to earn a little bit of interest on my money instead of depositing it with the bank that holds my mortgage and letting the bank earn the interest.

Share and Save

One way to save money is going to your grocery warehouse store with a friend. Not only will you have fun shopping together, you can also divide up the huge quantities you bought at good prices. Give her three of the jars of spaghetti sauce you bought in a six-pack, and she can give you three boxes of graham crackers from her purchase.

Another friendly swap can be done with magazines. Read the ones you subscribe to and then switch with a friend. And if you're wondering when you'll ever have time to read a magazine, put one or two in your car so you'll have them handy when you're waiting to pick up a child. Save *some* old magazines, but don't get carried away or you'll have piles of them. Children like to cut out pictures and glue them on paper to make their own art or use them in school projects.

A little creative swapping can provide both time with a friend and savings on your purchases.

One Woman's Trash...

When my husband and I were first married, we lived in an apartment in downtown Chicago. We parked our Volkswagen Rabbit in an underground garage, and one Saturday morning when we headed out to do some shopping, we noticed a full-size red metal popcorn machine in the garage near the garbage dumpster—the kind they make popcorn in at the movies. Wondering what it was doing there, we figured someone had needed help getting it up to his apartment and would soon be back to retrieve it. But why would someone want a big popcorn machine in an apartment? We kept admiring the machine and wishing we had a house and a basement and could keep the machine for our own children. After a few minutes, the building maintenance man walked by.

"I can't get over what people throw away nowadays," he said.

We were incredulous. "Throw away? Someone is throwing this away?"

"Yes. The guy asked me to put a special ticket on it for the garbage company so they'd take it on Tuesday."

My husband and I exchanged glances, and I asked the maintenance man if we could haul it away since it was being thrown out.

"Sure," he said. "You'll save me some work if you do."

We worked for 45 minutes loading it into the hatchback portion of our small car, drove it to my parents' house, and put it in their basement. We put an ad in the newspaper and sold the machine for $350 two weeks later.

While most of my finds have been far less valuable, I've learned that you just never know what good stuff you can find in someone else's trash.

Using Proper Tools

While my car was being repaired after a serious accident, the auto body shop let me use one of their cars during the repair period. I didn't have a proper ice scraper, and one rushed morning I scraped off the ice with the back of a hairbrush I had in the car. I know, it was *dumb*, and I put several scratches on the windshield of the loaner car in the process.

When I returned the loaner, I had to show Bruce at the body shop the scratches, telling him I'd pay for the damage I had done. My resources at that point were at an all-time low.

Bruce was kind about my foolishness and said I could just pay the deductible on the windshield, which he figured would be $100 or $250, which is what it was on most of his loaners. I knew I had to pay it and postpone other bills.

He got out the insurance cards for the loaner cars and looked through them for the car I had been using. He read them off as he went through the stack. Let's see…"$250, $100. Here's one for only $90 as a deductible. Oh, here's the one for the car you drove. That's funny, it's the only one with no deductible. You don't have to pay anything because it's a legitimate insurance claim."

Once again, God surprised me with a little gift.

Even though that day I was very glad that the car I had borrowed had no deductible, increasing your insurance deductibles is a way to save money because it lowers your insurance premiums. I recently raised my car insurance deductible and saved money on premiums, knowing I would have to pay more of the cost if I were in an accident. It's almost a form of self-insurance because I'm willing to pay more of the cost in the event of a claim.

Oh, and I did invest in a real ice scraper.

So I tell you, don't worry about everyday life—whether you have enough food, drink, and clothes. Doesn't life consist of more than food and clothing? Look at the birds. They don't need to plant or harvest or put food in barns because your heavenly Father feeds them. And you are far more valuable to him than they are.
—MATTHEW 6:25-26 NLT

Car Buying

When I get ready to buy a new car, I'm going to go to www.edmunds.com to find out how much I should pay for the car I choose. One woman I know used a price quote from this site to drive down the cost of her car purchase at a dealer.

Financial magazines occasionally publish an issue that focuses on the best cars, giving all sorts of helpful information on estimated repair costs, need for maintenance, specifications, prices, and comparisons between makes and models.

I'm not much of a bargain negotiator, but armed with the facts, I believe I can get a good price on my next car, especially if I get a used one that I have a mechanic check out first.

But I keep remembering the adage, "The cheapest car to own is the one I'm driving right now."

Fair-Weather Friends

Buying flowering annuals can be expensive, but they're so beautiful and colorful that I always get at least a few flats of impatiens, petunias, and begonias each spring. About four years ago at the end of the summer, some of my big geraniums were just too gorgeous to uproot and toss onto the compost pile, so I brought the pots inside and put them in my sunroom that stays sort of cool all winter. I decided to try bringing in some of the other flowering plants, reasoning that if they died I really hadn't lost anything except the time required to clean up a mess made by dead plants in the sunroom.

I brought in those tall spiky plants, vines, impatiens, and hanging baskets of begonias in addition to the geraniums. I didn't pay much attention to the plants over the winter, but I did water them at least every other week. They didn't look that great by the time the warm weather arrived in the spring, but they weren't dead, so I hauled them all back outside, trimmed off the wilted material, watered and fed them, and waited to see what would happen.

Some of the plants never came back, especially the impatiens, but many of the others revived and looked great in just a couple of weeks. So now every fall I bring in a bunch of plants and save quite a bit of money on annuals the next spring.

Safe but Sorry

My purse has been stolen twice—well, two different purses—both times taken out of my car when I was nearby, once at a neighbor's house and once at a playground. Yes, I finally learned to take my purse with me. On one of the occasions my car door was locked (at the neighbor's), and the other time I was pushing my three-year-old on a swing 30 feet from the unlocked car. That time I actually saw the thief get into my car, grab my purse, and run away as I yelled at him to give my purse back. For some reason, he didn't stop running and say, "Oh, excuse me. Is this yours? Here you go. I'm so sorry."

Of course, I was immediately struck with the thought, "What if Steve had been in the car and he had grabbed him too?" But I (almost) never left the children in the car, even for a few seconds.

Having my purse stolen the second time reminded me what a nuisance it is when that happens. It's scary and emotionally upsetting, but the nuisance of stolen credit cards and other belongings from your purse or wallet can really turn into a problem.

We've all heard of identity theft, and while I've never experienced that, the stolen purse episodes emphasized the importance of protecting my credit cards.

It's a good idea to photocopy your credit cards and driver's license by putting them all on a copy machine and copying both sides of each item. Keep the copies in a safe place in case your purse is stolen, and if it is, cancel your credit cards immediately (the toll-free numbers should be on the photocopies you made). Also, call the police and file a report, and call the three national credit reporting agencies and place a fraud alert on your name and social security number.

The agencies' phone numbers are:

Equifax: 1-800-525-6285
Experian: 1-888-397-3742
Trans Union: 1-800-680-7289

And even if you're like me, and it takes you a while to catch on to the dangers around us, please lock your car doors and take your purse *and* your kids with you.

$\wp$ $\wp$ $\wp$

Easy Cash Management

Using envelopes for cash expenses is a very old tactic, but I've found that it actually works if I stick to the program.

I have an envelope for each of several cash categories: groceries, gas, eating out, and miscellaneous. "Miscellaneous" covers a lot of territory, from dry cleaning to school supplies. But I divide up the budgeted amounts for each category, put the cash into each envelope each pay period, and then use cash for these purchases. The idea is, of course, that when the money runs out, I stop spending. I'm going to admit that I do use a credit card sometimes when faced with an empty envelope and an empty gas tank at the same time, but this system helps me stay on track with spending cash.

Recycling

When I was pregnant with my first child, my Sunday school class had a shower for me and gave me wonderful things, including a stroller and a car seat (lots of people went in together for those big items), and someone from the class offered to let me use her maternity tops. What a help that was—you don't plan on staying pumpkin-shaped for very long, so why buy those pretty and expensive maternity things you only wear for a few months?

I always tried to recycle my children's clothes by giving them to friends or relatives who had younger children than mine, and it seemed that someone with older kids was always donating outgrown things to me as well.

Whether you put recyclable items out at the curb or take them to a recycling center, many items can be recycled, from newspapers and cardboard to glassware and aluminum. Other household items, like old towels, make great car-washing rags, and old socks do a great job dusting.

I've learned to look at stuff with an analytical eye to see what additional use I might squeeze out of it.

Garage Sales

I know people who make hundreds of dollars every summer by hosting garage sales. But I am not one of them because of several humiliating experiences that always involved overpricing on my part. Each time I try it, I haul out all my stuff and just can't bear to put the tiny pricetags on them that my friends do. I hope people will bargain with me for the items, but if things are overpriced, they just go away immediately without dickering.

One year we had a neighborhood garage sale in which 20 homes participated. Across the street from my house, Denise earned $700; Mary took in $450. I earned $8 for a day-and-a-half of labor. I was offering everything from elegant track lighting to custom-made quilts and curtains. But as I hauled it all back into the garage after a disappointing day, I vowed never again to have another garage sale.

I've tried it a couple of times since, trying hard to offer low prices, but always coming away with a few dollars and a lot of junk left over. And while I'm talking about garage sales, I'm going to gripe a little. I hate it when I have something that cost $25 marked at 25 cents and someone asks, "Will you take a nickel for this?"

I know this is the way garage sales work, but I don't like it. When I shop at garage sales, I spend lavishly, paying the full quarter for a collection of hand-crocheted handkerchiefs.

So while Mary is earning $450 and Denise $700, I'm just going to take my junk, stomp into the house, and forget about it. If you, however, are a garage sale hostess with the right attitude, you, too, can make hundreds.

Hidden Expenses

When you're trying to cut costs of living, nothing is beyond a closer look, even something beautiful like a special tree in your yard. My friend Sue said she and her husband purchased a Spring Snow Crabapple tree for $300 several years ago as a sort of splurge for their yard. It is a lovely tree, but it is particularly susceptible to apple scab, and Sue and Tom are now spending $200 a year to have it sprayed. She pointed out that the upkeep on some possessions make them costly, like that white rug that has to be shampooed three times a year either professionally or by renting a machine yourself.

Big items, like boats and summer homes, are obviously expensive to maintain as well. So when you want to save money, look at the items that may require costly upkeep and consider doing without one or more of those high-maintenance items.

Tips on tightening your belt if you need to:

Reduce nonessentials:

Eating out

Starbucks

Number of phone lines

Cell phones

Entertainment, movies, etc.

Travel and vacations

Some clothes

Packaged or convenience foods

Nonessential driving

Long-distance calls

Extra car

Home decorating projects

Do-it-yourself repairs vs. hiring someone

Cable TV

Having company

Other places to save:

Mail vs. e-mail

Gift giving

Using coupons effectively

Grocery choices

Walking some places

Keeping lights and appliances off when not in use

Closing off unused rooms

Do-it-yourself hair color, perms, manicures

Cut kids' hair yourself

Look for sales

Less expensive ways to exercise

Do your own taxes

Do your own housecleaning, yard work

Buy fabric remnants and make your own curtains and pillows

Fit Is Fun

Guiding Your Family Toward Good Health

Today I joined a health club. I've been saving up and planning for when I could afford it. But if you knew me better, you'd know I'm not really much of a health club sort of gal. My husband and I belonged to a beautiful sports center for years. It was a five-minute walk from our house, or a 30-second drive. I regret now that I almost never used it. Oh, sure, we went over with the children and played volleyball in the sand, we took them swimming there, gave them tennis lessons and all, but I went to exercise myself probably ten times in the years we had the membership.

Now that I'm single and starting over financially, I've really been looking forward to joining a health club near my office. Today I went in, signed up, charged it to my credit card knowing I can pay it off soon, received my temporary membership card, and realized I had forgotten to bring suitable clothes for exercise. I had my picture taken and left, planning to return later to work out.

But on the way back to my house I noticed I was really hungry. The kids weren't home, so I stopped for a personal size pizza and ate it guiltily, promising I'll exercise the pizza off this evening and, if not then, tomorrow for sure.

I'm not going to waste this membership the way I did my last one, but as I threw away the pizza container, I realized that it's going to be a struggle to be sure I get there regularly and improve my eating habits as well. I surely can't stop for a snack on the way home from the health club. You know, rewarding myself for having exercised by picking up a few pieces of Fannie May candy.

Let's make a commitment to each other: We will exercise for at least 30 minutes three times a week and eat healthier as well. Together, we can do it. I just know it.

Time to Play

Recent studies indicate that we will receive health benefits from exercising at a moderate level of activity two or more times a week. You don't have to be a body builder or an aerobics enthusiast to improve your health. Moderate means activity that will use about 150 calories a day; for example, taking a brisk 30-minute walk every day. You can incorporate whatever kind of movement or exercise class you like into your life, and you can mix it up. Walk Monday, ride a bike Tuesday, climb stairs Wednesday, and so on. And even better—you can do the 30 minutes in three ten-minute chunks if you want to, making it easier than ever to help your health. The most important element is consistency, exercising regularly week in and week out, and that can be a challenge.

According to the National Center for Health Statistics, 32 percent of adults get some type of exercise two or more times a week, with 25 percent of adults classifying themselves as not physically active. Moderate activity includes playing volleyball for 45 minutes, raking leaves for 30 minutes, swimming laps for 20 minutes, playing basketball for 15–20 minutes, or running 1.5 miles in 15 minutes.

And if you are already regularly exercising at the moderate level, you can be even healthier by increasing the duration, intensity, or frequency of activity.

How to burn about 100 calories
(for a 120- to 150-pound person):

	Minutes Required
Clean/vacuum/mop floor	25–35
Wash dishes/iron	45–50
Mow lawn (self-propelled mower)	25–30
Mow lawn (manual mower)	12–15
Garden (digging or weeding)	10–20
Rake leaves	20–25
Wash/wax car or wash windows	20–25
Shovel snow	10–15
Blow snow	15–20
Walk (brisk)	15–25
Tennis	20–25
Golf (walk course)	20–25
Bicycle (5.5 mph)	20–30
Bicycle (9.4 mph)	15–20
Aerobics (medium intensity)	20–30

Take the Stairs

Did you know that by climbing stairs instead of taking the elevator you burn four calories for every ten steps you climb and exercise your muscles at the same time? I'm not suggesting that you use the stairs if you work in a 60-story skyscraper, but if it's just a couple of flights, go ahead. And when you multiply that calorie figure by the many trips mothers make up and down the stairs in any one day, taking the stairs is a good way to squeeze a little extra exercise into your day. It also helps build bone density because it is a weight-bearing exercise.

Other activities that burn calories while doing an enjoyable task are gardening (about 100 calories in 15 minutes), pushing the baby in the stroller or walking the dog (100 calories in 20 minutes), and mopping the kitchen floor (50 calories in 15 minutes). Okay, that last one is not so enjoyable, but it has to be done anyway.

How to help your kids get exercise:

- ✩ Set a good example. Be active yourself for at least 30 minutes a day.

- ✩ Limit amounts of time in front of TV or video games or computer.

- ✩ Encourage sports.

- ✩ Plan active vacations and family activities.

- ✩ Walk instead of drive sometimes, say, to the library or to get a newspaper.

⚹ Make some of the kids' chores physically active ones, like mowing the grass or raking leaves.

⚹ Take advantage of local park district activities.

⚹ Park at the far end of the parking lot.

Movers, Not Shakers

When I moved into my present house, I hired four strong, muscular high school boys at a reasonable hourly rate, packed everything myself, and rented a truck. I hired a special mover to move my baby grand piano and a couple of heavy pieces, but the teens did the rest. Besides earning money, they got a good workout that day.

Helping a friend move, paint, scrub, or garden is a good way to combine friendship and service with exercise. Do you have a friend who's about to move? Or paint her living room? By helping her you'll use some muscle groups you don't ordinarily use in addition to gaining that good feeling you get when you help someone else.

Delicacy in a Cup

I hate to admit it, but I'm addicted to coffee. I often wean myself down to one cup a day, but I really love my coffee with skim milk and honey in it. Honey, by the way, is a good source of antioxidants, especially dark honey like buckwheat honey. I used to drink my coffee black until I learned that caffeine reduces calcium absorption unless you drink it with whole, reduced fat, or skim milk.

After my divorce I gave up just about all my luxuries in order to save money and make ends meet, but the one I have kept until today is my Starbucks. I even splurge and buy the organic shade-grown coffee: one pound, ground for a cone drip. I don't buy the fancy drinks they make in the store, simply a tall regular with room for cream (or skim milk), but I love the smell and taste of the freshly ground stuff.

I treat spilled Starbucks grounds like an addict would his cocaine, carefully guarding each little grain and meticulously brushing it up and putting it back into the bag so I don't waste even one speck. But in order to offset whatever damage coffee might do, I always have a drink of water right alongside my cup. Because caffeine is a diuretic, drinking water with it prevents coffee from drying out my cells. And it also helps me not get the coffee jitters.

Super-Extra-Huge-Giant-Size, Please

I'm sure you've noticed that portion sizes in restaurants have gone from large to gargantuan in recent years. Some of the drinks from fast-food places are the size of my waste-basket, and food in restaurants is often served on what I use at home as a serving platter.

Because obesity is an increasingly widespread problem today, cutting down on portions helps. One woman I know brings a plastic container with her when she is eating out, and when her food comes, she puts half of it into her container immediately and sets it aside to take home. That way she's only tempted to eat half her meal at the restaurant. If you're too embarrassed to bring your own container, you could ask for a take-home container when you order your food and immediately put away half for later in one of those.

I heard on the radio that when food ingredients include "artificial flavors and/or sweeteners," they can contain chemicals created specifically to stimulate the appetite, making the eater want to consume more food. If this is true, it makes me angry to be manipulated into eating more than I need so that someone will make an extra dollar.

But in the end it's my responsibility to decide what goes (or doesn't go) into my mouth. Halving portions is one way to avoid weight gain.

Get an Oil Change

Use olive oil in recipes, even in cakes and other sweets, substituting it for other vegetable oils or butter. You won't taste a bit of difference and will have a healthier cake. Olive oil is a monounsaturated fat containing antioxidants and a high concentration of squalene, both known to be cancer fighters. It also provides selenium, a much-needed trace mineral.

Extra virgin olive oil, the top of the line, must have been judged to have perfect flavor and odor by a panel of experts and have a certain level of acidity. It is the least processed and considered to be the healthiest of the various grades. But extra virgin olive oil may still be chemically processed or extracted and is not necessarily "organic."

The use of olive oil in the diet has been linked positively with blood thinning and a reduction in the blood's clotting ability, meaning fewer heart attacks. Studies have shown that individuals whose diets were enriched with olive oil for at least three weeks had a lower clotting factor than those whose diets included other kinds of fats and oils.

A diet rich in olive oil has also been linked with lower fat deposits on the walls of arteries, which can lead to high blood pressure, strokes, and heart attacks. Olive oil consumption is also being linked to lowered rates of certain types of cancer.

The Mediterranean diet—heavy in tomatoes and other vegetables as well as olive oil—seems to be a wise choice for healthy eating.

I Am What I Eat

I hate to admit it, but my cholesterol level has been high at my last two wellness screenings. The reason I hate to admit it is because I richly deserve the high readings—I do like my butter, mayo, and sweets. Last year my doctor said that because I'm not really overweight, he would give me a year to try to bring it down with diet, or else he would prescribe a cholesterol-lowering medication. Fortunately, I have a high reading on the good kind of cholesterol, the HDL type.

So I have tried to increase my consumption of fruits and vegetables and make my protein sources largely chicken, fish, and soy, although I love a good burger occasionally. And I did manage to bring it down from 260 to 248 this year, not a stellar accomplishment, but a step in the right direction. I don't know if the doctor will be suitably impressed with this small improvement or whether he'll insist on my taking the medication immediately. Oh, for more self-discipline.

Three steps to lower your risk of heart disease and stroke:*

1. Don't smoke cigarettes, cigars, or pipes, and don't chew tobacco. Smoking among adults has decreased by 40 percent since 1965.

2. Reduce the fat in your diet and use monounsaturated fats like olive oil or grapeseed oil in place of other fats and oils, to lower cholesterol and help lose weight.

3. Get regular exercise, even 30 minutes a day of walking or gardening, to increase circulation, metabolism, and muscle mass. Exercise also helps lower high blood pressure and high cholesterol.

* Check with your doctor before beginning any new diet or exercise plan.

Just the Flax, Ma'am

My cousin Sandra gave me a book called *The Fat Flush Plan* by Ann Louise Gittleman.[3] Even the title sounds good, doesn't it? I read the book, loved it, and started the plan. I stuck to it for three weeks, lost weight, and felt great.

I wish I could say I stayed with it, but as usual, I lapsed back into my old ways of eating.

But I did take a couple of parts of the plan with me into my present eating patterns, such as eating ground flax seeds and/or flax seed oil every day. As the book says to do, I mix the ground seeds into a mixture of unsweetened cranberry juice and water and add the oil to a fruit smoothie consisting of fresh or frozen fruit, 2 tablespoons of soy protein powder, and a cup of the cranberry-water mixture. Apparently flax helps rid the body of toxins, improving liver function and lowering cholesterol.

Nuts About Nuts

One of my mother's most delicious recipes is her pecan pie recipe. She always ordered pecans fresh from Georgia, and she ordered them by what seemed like the ton. Every year during November, several crates of pecans in one- or two-pound bags would be delivered to our house. Mother would start distributing them to her friends and relatives, and she would use them for the holidays, making fruitcake (we all hated it), fudge (we all loved it), those little pecan ball cookies rolled in powdered sugar, and her wonderful pecan pie.

One year I entered my pecan pie in our Sunday school class's Fourth of July pie contest and won. But when I got home, after basking in the glory all afternoon, I realized that I routinely use a store-bought crust for pecan pies, even though I make them from scratch for other kinds, such as blueberry.

I had to call the person who had conducted the contest and admit that I had used a "fake" crust. You would think she would have said, "Oh, don't worry about it. I'm sure you meant no harm." But instead she said, "I'm glad your conscience made you confess this."

I figured she just wished *she* had won the contest.

Research shows that eating a few pecans may be as beneficial to your blood vessels as cooking with cholesterol-friendly olive oil. Pecans are high in fat, but it's mostly the heart-healthy kind of fat. One tablespoon has 45 calories, that is, unless you make them into a pie!

Make Mine Grapes

Everyone is talking about the health benefits of drinking a glass or two of wine a day. Now this advice is fine if wine doesn't tire you out, depress you, or make you want to drink four more glasses. I must admit to being in that category, so I am wary of the wine-for-health craze.

But apparently you can eat grapes and get the same benefit that you get from drinking wine.[4] Both wine and grapes contain resveratrol (try pronouncing that one!), a compound believed to be good for both cancer prevention and heart health. Organic grapes have the highest levels of resveratrol because they have not been treated with pesticides.

> **Big baby steps:** Healthy adults can reduce their risk of heart attack and stroke by taking one baby aspirin every day. Again, check with your doctor before beginning a program such as this.

I *Knew* Pizza Was Healthy

Adding tomato paste to your diet helps your lungs stay healthy because it contains both vitamin C and magnesium, two nutrients thought to benefit the lungs. Tomato paste or puree is richer in these nutrients than tomato sauce or tomato juice and can be added to many foods. These foods also provide beta carotene.

According to www.sciencenews.org, lycopene is a little known carotenoid that gives tomatoes and other fruits and vegetables their rich color, but it also plays an important role in eliminating free radicals that cause disease and aging.

Interestingly, tomato paste is thought to contain more of these valuable ingredients than fresh tomatoes.

So don't feel guilty anymore about serving your family pizza! It's good for them, especially if it doesn't contain processed meats.

The Eyes Will Have It

Protect your family members' vision by serving spinach often. Research shows that antioxidants found in spinach may protect the retina and retard the development of macular degeneration that can cause blindness in the elderly. Other foods that include these antioxidants are oranges, zucchini, corn, grapes, and kiwi.

My children all like spinach, either in salads or cooked with a little butter on it. I usually plant spinach seeds in the spring, but I need to water them faithfully, weed around them, and hope that the rabbits don't eat the plants before we can. I stay on the lookout for rabbits with big, muscular limbs like Popeye's arms, knowing that they're probably on the prowl for the spinach in my yard.

Another way to protect your vision is wearing UV-blocking sunglasses, which are believed to protect against damaging rays that can cause macular degeneration and cataracts.

Salmon and Soy

No, I'm not suggesting eating them together. But the health benefits of both foods are impressive.

Soy is thought to help prevent breast cancer, lower cholesterol, and help with weight loss by providing high quality, low-fat protein. Although I haven't acquired a taste for tofu yet, I have recently embarked on a soy shake program with a friend because a mutual acquaintance has some pretty compelling anecdotal evidence it has worked to reduce his blood cholesterol level significantly in just a few months. The shakes are a bit pricey and very sweet, but we're giving them a try.

I also try to eat salmon frequently, and I simply put it in a covered pan with a little water and add lemon juice, spices, and teriyaki or soy sauce, whatever I have. It's usually a good choice to order in a restaurant, too, like blackened salmon salad or salmon with grilled vegetables.

Strong Bones and Teeth and...Ovaries?

I love dairy products, don't you? What could be better than a delicious hunk of cheddar cheese with a bite of a succulent fresh pear? Or just about anything slathered with melted butter? (I'm proud to say that I never followed any of those margarine fads; I always stuck with the real thing even before they knew that butter was healthier than margarine.)

The good news is that calcium in dairy products may help protect women from ovarian cancer. Studies have shown that women who consume calcium-rich dairy products, including low-fat and nonfat milk, have about half the risk of ovarian cancer compared with women who ate very little dairy.

The bad news is that it needs to be low-fat or nonfat foods because of cholesterol and weight gain, but even that's not all bad. I've become perfectly accustomed to skim milk, and I've learned that fresh fruits and vegetables like spinach and oranges also provide large amounts of calcium.

Two years ago I had a bone-density screening that showed a teensy-weensy bit of bone-thinning. The doctor recommended that I begin taking 1600 milligrams of calcium daily, so I bought some large calcium tablets (400 milligrams each) and took four of them every day.

The next year I had the bone-density screen repeated, and the fellow who administered the test showed me the results, adding, "You have the bones of a 30-year-old."

Calcium also helps increase the good cholesterol (HDL) in your blood.

I was delighted to learn that you can reverse the beginnings of osteoporosis quite easily, and I really like having the bones of a 30-year-old.

Cooking Glass

I'm sort of fussy about some things (it runs in the family—my brother wipes out every glass he drinks out of for fear of lint!), and I never use nor allow my children to use plastic in the microwave, whether it's a plastic container or plastic wrap, even the ones that say they're microwave-safe.

I prefer glass containers, bowls, or plates, and I put a glass lid over messy foods so they won't splatter all over the inside of the microwave. I felt vindicated in my eccentricity when a friend sent me an e-mail to the effect that someone had found carcinogens in foods microwaved in plastic.

Staying Sharp

My mother had Alzheimer's disease, and, frankly, I fear getting it someday, so I try to read up on ways to strengthen my brain in hopes of avoiding it. So far I've found that vitamin E and also folate help keep the mind sharp, in addition to doing active mental activities like crossword puzzles and reading. Avocados and nuts contain vitamin E, but I also take a daily supplement. Folate is also believed to help prevent colon cancer. And I take B-complex vitamins to aid neurotransmitter function, which helps the brain process nerve impulses. Another preventative measure is to increase your intake of unsaturated fat (olive oil) and reduce your intake of saturated fat.

Early research indicates that curcumin, an ingredient in curry and cumin spices, may help inhibit the buildup in the brain of certain proteins that have been associated with Alzheimer's disease. Curcumin also is believed to possess powerful antioxidant and anti-inflammatory properties.

Another weapon in the arsenal against this disease is lifelong learning. If you keep your mind active by learning new things, you can actually grow new brain synapses.

Rare Air

I purchased an electronic air cleaner for my furnace, partly because I fervently hoped it would help me not have to dust so often, but also because I want to keep the air quality in my home healthful. Of course, I have to clean the filter in order for it to be effective, so if I forget to do it for months, it renders the device ineffective. So that's something I try to do monthly.

Another air quality issue is carbon monoxide, an odorless gas that, when present at certain levels, can cause moderate to severe illness or even death.

According to the Consumer Product Safety Commission, 7000 people go to the emergency room and 200 people die annually from this poisonous gas. Keeping your furnace, fireplace, and chimney in good shape is important in addition to installing the carbon monoxide detectors at least 15 feet away from a gas furnace or water heater. In a hallway is a good location if you have an electrical outlet there. The detectors will show whether there are unsafe levels of carbon monoxide present in your home, sounding an alarm if the levels are elevated. I have one detector in the living room and one in a bedroom. Of course, smoke detectors on every floor are important as well. All detecting devices should be vacuumed monthly and have their batteries changed annually.

Water, Water Every Day

About ten years ago my husband and I opened a water store. It was a lovely store with a mesmerizing water wall containing bubbles that floated up seemingly to nowhere in a fascinating way. We sold bottled water from around the world and water purification equipment. We thought it was an idea whose time had come, but in less than a year, the business went broke. People loved the store, but you need to sell many, many bottles of Gerolsteiner or San Pelegrino at a dollar something each in order to pay the rent.

So we lost some money and closed the business. But we learned a lot about water, and I still insist on cleaning my drinking water with a reverse osmosis system. I'm sure there are other good ways to do it too, but that is my personal favorite. I don't just drink any old water from anywhere.

I take my own water to work, as many people do, and for a long time I filled up a reusable quart bottle and froze it overnight because I like my water cold. But it took quite a while during the workday for the ice to melt enough to really be able to drink it except in small sips, so someone suggested freezing just half a bottle of water and then filling up the rest of the bottle with water in the morning. It works great, and I have cold, but unfrozen, water to enjoy all day! I aim to drink 64 ounces, or eight glasses, a day to improve physical and mental performance and to help in weight loss.

I learned something surprising recently. There is a condition called "water intoxication" that occurs when massive amounts of water are consumed. It can be fatal. For me, getting down the 64 ounces is hard enough to accomplish, so I don't think I'm in danger of getting "drunk" on water.

A Very Important Date

Preventative medicine is the best kind. Be sure to schedule and keep the appointment for your annual Pap test and breast exam, as well as dental appointments and other medical services you may need because of age or family history.

Medical studies are indicating that certain screening tests can vastly improve early detection and treatment of many diseases, such as heart disease, diabetes, and cancer. Making sure you and your family have the appropriate medical care is essential in keeping your family fit.

It's easy when the children are babies and they go in every few months—carried in your arms—for their checkups. As the children grow, it's a lot harder to schedule appointments around everyone's sports and school activities and get them there, but we moms need to make health checkups and screenings a top priority because there are few gifts as precious as good health.

Good news: With the emphasis on healthier living, including prevention efforts and improvements in early detection, U.S. death rates from heart disease and stroke have decreased by 60 percent since 1950.

Sunning Safely

I am rather fair-skinned with a red-headed, freckled sister, but my ex-husband was dark olive-skinned, and two of my three children inherited beautiful, smooth skin that deeply tans with the slightest exposure to the sun. My son Steve is fairer, like me, and, although he tans, he does not become nearly as dark as his siblings.

But I still slathered all three with sunblock with a sun protection factor (SPF) of 15 or higher whenever they were out in the sun building sand castles, swimming, or even playing in a sunny park. We didn't know back in my childhood that sunburns could cause skin cancer years later, and I can remember a few really bad ones. Fortunately, so far, no problems.

I do try to wear a hat and UV-protective sunglasses while gardening in my sun-drenched yard, and I use sunblock myself if I'm outside.

Kids Are Fast

When my daughter was about ten months old, I found her sitting on the floor of our pantry with an empty plastic bag that had previously contained wheat berries that are so good for you if you cook them and serve them like a round and crunchy kind of oatmeal. She had crawled to the pantry, pulled the bag off the bottom shelf, and dumped the whole thing out at her feet. She sat there smiling at me and saying "bersie."

Now this was my first child, and you know that mothers' eyes are glued to that first one the way you can't stop watching TV during a national crisis. I watched her constantly and carefully, but she still managed to pull something down from a shelf and dump it out.

This experience made me double-check the safety mechanisms I had put on the cabinet doors where cleaning chemicals were kept. It takes a child only a few moments to get into something that could really hurt her.

To keep your little ones safe, be sure you have those little electrical outlet covers all plugged in, install stair gates to prevent falls down stairs, keep all chemicals and medicines way out of reach or, even better, locked up, and be sure there is no old flaking paint that could contain lead that your child might ingest.

Fill 'er Up, Please

Are you a "half full" or a "half empty" person? Do you tend to look at half a glass of water and see what's good about it (it's half full) or do you tend to see the problem (it's half empty)? I believe that, with practice, we can go from being pessimists to optimists.

Optimists handle stress better than pessimists. That seems obvious, but it's important to remember that our mental outlook makes a significant impact on our health. Research indicates that optimistic people make and keep friendships more easily, and having social support is crucial in mental health.

The Prayer Health Connection

Numerous studies have indicated that one's spiritual life has a strong connection to her ability to heal. Does prayer have the power to heal? No, prayer doesn't have that power, but the God to whom we pray does. I'm sure you've heard, as I have, of miraculous answers to prayers for healing, but other times the healing takes place in heaven after this life is concluded.

The medical community has observed that when a patient has a strong connection to others who pray for her, and when the patient is also a person of prayer, she is more likely to recover. The reasons are not fully known, but for those of us who have seen prayer answered, we know prayer is powerful!

Many studies make a religion-health link, and some of the factors involved include lifestyle choices. When people believe that God gave them a wonderful gift of their human body and gave them the job of taking good care of it as a steward, they try to eat healthier and avoid harmful behaviors like addictions.

Another of the many wonderful benefits of knowing and loving God is answered prayer, whether the request concerns a health need or anything else—one more reason to let all our requests be made known to God.

Made for a Purpose

Mary is a mother, a grandmother, a wife, and an artist. She makes beautiful decoupaged flowerpots, watering cans, and buckets, using a laborious process.

First, she paints and antiques a plain, clay flowerpot. Then she uses a sharp knife to carefully cut out several flowers or bumblebees or birds from wrapping paper she collects from all over the world. She glues the paper designs onto the pot, smoothing out all the bubbles, and then applies up to seven coats of varnish.

This process creates quite a mess in her kitchen, which doubles as her studio. Scraps of paper, paintbrushes, drop cloths, and sandpaper litter the counter and the floor. She looks at the finished pot a little disappointedly. Amid the rubble, it looks forlorn and plain to her.

Is it really worth it? she wonders.

But when she sees that same pot in a lovely display in a big department store that sells her work, the pot looks different. It's now where it was meant to be, out of the messy kitchen and in a beautiful setting. Her artwork looks beautiful too.

We are God's artwork, but sometimes, amid the rubble of problems and difficulties in our lives, we don't feel like a lovely masterpiece. We feel ordinary and dull. But as we fulfill God's plan and purpose for our lives, we look different because we are where we were designed to be. And ultimately, we'll be "displayed" in heaven, without blot or blemish, in the surroundings we were meant for.

All mothers need a creative outlet, and the choice of yours is up to you. Perhaps you write songs, write letters to missionaries, sing in the choir, play the violin, paint oil paintings, draw with chalk, cook gourmet dishes, make floral wreaths, invent computer programs, lead a book discussion group, or participate in an investment club. Whatever you do that brings you joy or helps you learn something new or expresses your thoughts and feelings is, to me, a creative outlet.

Studies have shown that mental and emotional health is improved by participating in creative activities, either alone or with others. So dust off your oil paints and spend a few minutes today doing something that expresses who you are.

> For we are God's masterpiece. He has created us anew in
> Christ Jesus, so that we can do the good things he
> planned for us long ago.
> —EPHESIANS 2:10 NLT

God's masterpiece. Do you feel like a masterpiece? Sometimes moms feel more like messes than masterpieces at the end of a demanding day. Some days we barely have time to get everyone—including ourselves—where we all need to be and make sure the family's needs are met. But when we realize that in God's eyes we are beautiful works of art, our lives and our efforts take on new meaning. The work we do every day is something he planned for us long ago. Take a minute to thank God that you are indeed his lovely artwork, highly valuable, and significant.

Food and Mood

I am a person who has struggled with depression. Years ago, during a difficult time in my marriage, I took a downward emotional spiral that I thought would kill me. I became obsessed with painful thoughts, and they almost paralyzed me. Fortunately, I soon realized I needed professional help for my depression. I had three young children to care for, and I needed to be able to function.

I went to the doctor, was prescribed an antidepressant, and was referred to a counselor to help me deal with some life issues. After two weeks on the medication, the torturous thinking abated, and I was able to handle my situation once again. I stayed on the medication for the next ten years through some very turbulent life waters, trying to get off a couple of times but finding each time that I needed to continue it. Along with everyone who loved me, I was very thankful to have medication that helped me so much.

Finally, with my doctor's supervision and instructions, I weaned myself off, and then I really began to learn the importance of what I eat. I had become very sensitive to sugar, and a delicious chocolate malt, a big piece of cake, or even one glass of wine resulted in depression.

My homeopathic practitioner friend, Chana, gave me vitamins, essential oils, and homeopathic remedies, and she said I must eat well if I'm going to go without the medication. I've discovered that if I eat protein with three meals every day and avoid sugar in all its forms (I still have a little honey in my coffee), as well as white processed flour, which turns to sugar in the bloodstream, I am less depressed. I can have a small dessert occasionally if I have just eaten protein.

After the deaths of my sister and my mother in one month's time, I went back on the medication after a five-month break, and with proper eating, I feel great again.

I encourage my children to watch their sugar consumption and eat sweets only after eating protein. If you experience emotional ups and downs, you might try taking a careful look at what you eat and how it affects you. And if you feel really bad and it doesn't go away, please see your doctor immediately.

Chill!

The pace of life today obviously can be stressful. The *Harvard Medical School Family Health Guide* suggests that when we experience stress symptoms such as those listed below, it's time to change our mental focus by singing or praying to get our mind off our worries. Slow, deep breathing, where you fill up your lower abdomen first and then the chest area and releasing air through the mouth until it feels like it's all squeezed out, is another stress-reliever. If you or someone in your family complains of any of these symptoms continuously, it's time to see the doctor because they can be signs of depression or anxiety that are very treatable:

- ❀ headache
- ❀ back pain
- ❀ indigestion
- ❀ tight neck and shoulders
- ❀ stomach pain
- ❀ racing heart
- ❀ sweaty palms
- ❀ restlessness
- ❀ sleep problems
- ❀ dizziness
- ❀ loss of appetite

Tennis, Anyone?

Do you ever wonder why you can't just do it God's way since he's always right? Take problems like worry and anxiety and fear and all those other awful emotions that God doesn't want us to carry around. I know he'll help me with them if I ask him, but giving my worries to God is a lot like watching a tennis match for me: my head goes back and forth, from side to side, as I send that hot worry topic over his way, then I take it back and start agonizing over it again. I realize he'll take care of it for me, so I shoot it back, and later find myself chewing on it again.

Worry and stress are harmful to our health. According to Medline Plus, a website of the National Institutes of Health (www.medlineplus.gov), the physical effects of these emotions include racing heartbeat, pulsing blood, tensed muscles, undigested food stuck in the stomach, and elevated levels of hormones coursing through the circulatory system, possibly leading to hypertension. Too much stress also affects the immune system, weakening it and making us more susceptible to illness.

Not only that, but worrying doesn't fix anything. There may be a fine line between problem solving and worrying, but a mental picture I like to bring to mind is one of my gorgeous Asiatic lilies, standing stately in the yard, calm, elegant, and comfortable with herself. A breeze makes her shudder a little bit, but she just lets it jostle her for a minute, and then she's steady again, head held high and smiling at the sun.

I don't know whether the lilies in Matthew 6 were Asiatic lilies, but God said to look at them and notice how carefree and settled they are, and then go and do likewise.

It may seem to be a difficult habit to cultivate, but God promises his care in exchange for our worry.

✍ ✍ ✍

> Why are you worried about clothing? Observe how the lilies of the field grow; they do not toil nor do they spin, yet I say to you that even Solomon in all his glory did not clothe himself like one of these.
> —Matthew 6:28-29

Tuning Up

Singing is healthy. I love the Three Tenors, and in my car I often crank them up and sing along with *Missa Solemnis,* even though I don't speak any foreign languages except *un poco* of Spanish and the pig latin my sister and I mastered in unior-jay igh-hay.

But singing is an emotional release and a mood enhancer. Of course, if all you sing are those sad ballads about who left whom, it might not cheer you up as much as a sweet little rendition of "This Little Light of Mine" with your kids.

I have sung in church choirs, and I got my choral start back in high school with Miss Barbara Barnes, who was a fine musician. We performed musicals every year, and one of my favorites was *My Fair Lady.* I never had starring roles—no matter how many hours I spent at home in front of the mirror fantasizing about being the lead—but in this production I was one of the Ascot ladies, and we wore hats and pretty, old-fashioned floor-length dresses and carried parasols.

I'll never forget the searing look in Miss Barnes' eyes when I walked on stage two minutes late because I had been backstage chatting. I was supposed to be seated primly with three other Ascot ladies and four Ascot gentlemen. But when the curtain came up, I was missing. I tried to walk out in character, but she turned steely eyes on me, and I've never forgotten it.

But I didn't feel bad enough about it to stop singing.

Calm in a Crisis

All three of my children required emergency stitches during their childhoods. My daughter fell and hit her forehead on the edge of the dishwasher door on the same day the Challenger crashed in 1986. She was less than a year old.

My older son, Andrew, cut the area between his upper lip and his nose on the end of a metal scooter handle, and the little guy, Steve, fell into a door on a vacation at Disneyland, sustaining a vertical cut through his eyebrow. Then there was the time Steve jumped up on his dad while he was carrying fishing poles and got three fish hooks stuck in his poor little palm.

Today's bit of advice involves taking as many precautions as are reasonable and then forgiving yourself when the inevitable accident happens. I'm happy to report that all three survived their stitches, although at the time I was sick about each injury.

I remember that my main goal on those days was to stay calm, comforting, and loving to minimize the child's fear and pain. I knew that having a panicky, upset parent would have just made the experience worse for the child.

And these experiences remind me that on my emergency days, my Parent is calm, comforting, and loving, seeing me through each crisis and setting me back on my feet.

❧   ❧   ❧

Taking the Long View

One of the healthiest things you can do for your mental outlook is to look up from your work and peer far out into the distance. This not only rests your eyes, it can also have a calming effect for your soul.

When we had our vacation home, the drive out there provided long vistas and views of wooded hills and flat plains. I could look far off into the distance, and it always gave me a new perspective. It's pretty flat where I live now, and all I can see when I look out my windows are the houses in my neighborhood or my yard. I like looking at those things just fine, but there's no opportunity for a long view.

Occasionally I'll go visit someone who lives somewhere that requires a nice drive and look off into the distance (being careful to watch the road ahead of me most of the time), and I find it refreshing to get the long view once in a while.

Of course, getting the long view of life helps too. While my lifetime is but a vapor in God's timetable, he has a glorious plan for what each of us will be doing throughout eternity.

I'll conclude with some of my favorite verses that I hope will encourage you as much as they do me, Jeremiah 29:11-13, " 'For I know the plans that I have for you,' declares the LORD, 'plans for welfare and not for calamity to give you a future and a hope. Then you will call upon Me and come and pray to Me, and I will listen to you. And you will seek

Me and find Me, when you search for Me with all your heart.' "

❧   ❧   ❧

I must say goodbye for now, and I truly hope you've enjoyed reading this book even a fraction as much as I've enjoyed writing it. I hope you've laughed a few times, come away with a few new ideas, and, most importantly, have realized that your mothering is critically important work, one with eternal consequences. I also hope you feel a little lighter, having shed some of the guilt that many of us lug around.

Thank you for listening to what I've had to say. My best wishes as you love your family and do your work. May God bless your efforts.

Please stay in touch with me by visiting my website at www.momsarecool.com.

Barbara

Index

Notes

1. Michael F. Roizen, M.D., *RealAge: Are You as Young as You Can Be?* (New York: HarperCollins, 1999), p. 38.

2. Richard Ferber, M.D., *Solve Your Child's Sleep Problems* (New York: Simon & Schuster, 1985).

3. Ann Louise Gittleman, M.S., C.N.S., *The Fat Flush Plan* (New York: McGraw Hill, 2002).

4. www.realage.com

How to Contact the Author:

Barbara Mang
c/o Harvest House Publishers
990 Owen Loop North
Eugene, OR 97402
or www.momsarecool.com

More Great Books from Harvest House Publishers

10-MINUTE TIME OUTS FOR MOMS
Grace Fox

This gathering of insightful devotions from author and mother Grace Fox encourages you to communicate with God throughout your day. Grace's homespun stories and Scripture-based prayers provide inspiration and practical guidance to help you maintain a vital connection with God. You'll discover refreshment and comfort as you spend each time-out with God.

KEEP IT SIMPLE FOR MOMS ON THE GO
Emilie Barnes

How can I ever cross everything off my "to-do" list? The answer is "keep it simple." And here is a collection of creative ways to help every mom simplify her life. Emilie's faithful readers will love her newest collection of great advice...especially if they're "moms on the go"!

ONE-MINUTE PRAYERS™ FOR BUSY MOMS
Harvest House Publishers

Designed to serve the pace and needs of everyday life, *One–Minute Prayers™ for Busy Moms* refreshes women with simple prayers and inspirational verses when they need it most. For women who rarely take time for themselves, this book offers stepping stones to a deeper prayer life.

PEANUT BUTTER KISSES AND MUD PIE HUGS
Becky Freeman

For years author Becky Freeman chose the pattern on furniture and bedspreads for its ability to blend in with peanut butter and jelly. As her kids have grown, so have her tales about the warmth and laughter that family life brings. Nestled among the frogs and snowcones and football practices, readers will discover little lessons about God and His love for His children of all ages.